Functionalism and Interdependence

THE CREDIBILITY OF INSTITUTIONS, POLICIES AND LEADERSHIP
A Series funded by the Hewlett Foundation
Kenneth W. Thompson, *Series Editor*

I. Ideas and Approaches to Politics and Foreign Policy

Volume 1: Moralism and Morality in Politics and Diplomacy
Kenneth W. Thompson

Volume 2: The American Approach to Foreign Policy: A Pragmatic Perspective
Cecil V. Crabb, Jr.

Volume 3: Functionalism and Interdependence
John Eastby

Volume 4: American Approaches to World Affairs
I. L. Claude

II. Institutions and Public Attitudes

Volume 5: The Media
Kenneth W. Thompson (ed.)

Volume 6: The Private Sector
J. Wilson Newman

Volume 7: The President and the Public: Rhetoric and National Leadership
Kathy B. and Craig Allen Smith (eds.)

Volume 8: Law and Diplomacy: The Plimpton Papers
Mrs. Francis T.P. Plimpton

Volume 9: Bureaucracy and Statesmanship
Robert A. Strong

III. Consensus and Public Policy

Volume 10: The Last European Peace Conference: Paris 1946— Conflict of Values
Stephen Kertesz

Volume 11: Foreign Policy and Domestic Consensus
Richard Melanson and Kenneth W. Thompson (eds.)

Volume 12: Consensus: Issues and Problems
Michael Joseph Smith and Kenneth W. Thompson (eds.)

Volume 13: McCarthyism and Consensus?
William B. Ewald, Jr.

Volume 14: Consensus and the American Mission
Brian Klunk

Volume 15: The United States Acquires the Philippines: Consensus vs. Reality
Louis J. Halle

IV. Leaders and Credibility

Volume 16: Essays on Leadership: Comparative Insights
Kenneth W. Thompson (ed.)

Volume 17: American Moral and Political Leadership in the Third World
Kenneth W. Thompson (ed).

Volume 18: U.S. Leadership in Asia and the Middle East
Kenneth W. Thompson (ed.)

Volume 19: Winston S. Churchill: Philosopher and Statesman
Michael Fowler

Volume 20: Institutions and Leadership: Prospects for the Future
Kenneth W. Thompson (ed.)

Functionalism and Interdependence

The Credibility of Institutions, Policies and Leadership
Volume 3

JOHN EASTBY

With a Preface by Kenneth W. Thompson

University Press of America
Lanham • New York • London

Copyright © 1985 by

University Press of America,® Inc.

4720 Boston Way
Lanham, MD 20706

3 Henrietta Street
London WC2E 8LU England

Co-published by arrangement with
The White Burkett Miller Center of Public Affairs,
University of Virginia

Library of Congress Cataloging in Publication Data

Eastby, John, 1953-
  Functionalism and interdependence.

  (The Credibility of institutions, policies and
leadership; v. 3)
  1. International organization. 2. Functionalism
(Social sciences) I. Title. II. Series.
JX1954.E35   1985   327   85-3133
ISBN 0-8191-4418-5 (alk. paper)
ISBN 0-8191-4419-3 (pbk. : alk. paper)

Contents

Preface

A host of observers have described contemporary international society as an interdependent world. Nations are linked to one another by bonds of trade and commerce, culture and history, social and scientific relations and the need to work together to survive. People to people programs cross frontiers and science, we are told, knows no national boundaries. The most urgent problems confronting the world can no longer be solved within national boundaries. These include the threat of nuclear war but also the population explosion, environmental deterioration and world food production. The scope and character of the world's problems have in a sense made the nation state obsolete.

These facts have led some of our ablest thinkers to put forward ideas and theories to cope with these problems. Some have elaborated theories of transnational relations. Others like Joseph Nye and Robert Keohane have written about interdependence. The British thinker David Mitrany propounded an approach called functionalism intended to demonstrate that overlapping social and economic interests concerning urgent problems might lead to an erosion of sovereignty.

John Eastby has contributed an important study of functionalism and interdependence to the Hewlett Series of the Miller Center on Institutions and Leadership. Part One of the Series examines ideas and approaches to politics and international relations. Quite appropriately, Eastby's volume falls within this part of the Series.

Interdependence is indeed a reality but its effectiveness and workings depend on those residual factors of national interest that limit its application. Dr. Eastby traces the core ideas of functionalism as enunciated by Mitrany, various post-Mitrany interpretations by thinkers such as Hans J. Morgenthau and I. L. Claude and changes in the approach in response to new problems.

No one has discussed the theory and practice of functionalism with greater analytical rigor than Eastby. His book makes a lasting contribution to our understanding.

Kenneth W. Thompson
The White Burkett Miller
Center of Public Affairs

Introduction

My purpose in the first section of this discussion is to re-evaluate functionalism. My method is first, to establish what I consider to be the basic tenets of functional theory with particular reference to David Mitrany. The following chapters constitute a review of what I consider to be the most important discussions of the theory. In my selection will be found a number of authors who have classically been termed, and occasionally termed themselves, realists. Hans J. Morgenthau is typically considered to be the primary exponent of realism (a perspective which is now mistakenly identified with state-centrism). Reinhold Niebuhr, who provides the basis for my own evaluation of functionalism, is again considered a realist. Finally, Kenneth W. Thompson, whose criteria for evaluation provide the framework for the last section of this publication is also considered to be a realist. It was the quality and character of their reflections on the subject at hand that led me to these particular writers, not the fact that they are realists or state-centrists. Much the same may be said of my examination of Inis L. Claude and James P. Sewell though the work of neither analyst could easily be fit into any category even if one wished to do so. At one point Ernst B. Haas could have been classed with the group of analysts known as neo-functionalist. Perhaps his work might still be classified with the scientific and behavioral movement which has swept through political science. At the very least one might say that, until recently, Haas was less concerned with the relationship between political behavior and the values of the political analyst than our other commentators have been. We may say as well that Haas' attempt to use functionalism as a tool for changing the way international relations are studied distinguishes him from the other commentators.

None of the above authors could be considered thoroughly committed adherents to Mitrany's political approach. In fact, out of the *corpus* of each author's major works the direct discussion of functionalism generally fills a small space. Morgenthau only devotes a few pages to the discussion of functionalism. Without offering a bibliography, it may be noted that the remainder of *Politics Among Nations*[1] offers a comprehensive analysis of international relations as they have developed to the present time, while other of his works aim more directly to influence the policy debate on the major issues of the day.[2] *Scientific Man Versus Power Politics*[3] is most nearly described as a philosophy of politics.

Claude addresses functionalism in *Swords Into Plowshares*[4] but the overall content of the text can hardly be said to concentrate on functionalism. *Power and International Relations*[5] examines methods of managing power in international relations, concentrating on the balance of power, collective security and world government as possible methods for doing so. *National Minorities*[6] examines the problem raised for states and the state system by the co-existence of distinct cultural groups which do not correspond in their geographic distribution with the territorial boundaries of states. *The Changing United Nations*[7] and many of Claude's articles examine the legal, institutional and political aspects of the process of international organization and are not devoted in a strict sense to the teaching of or investigation of functionalism. Sewell's major work since his *Functionalism and World Politics*,[8] *UNESCO and World Politics*,[9] officially abandoned the functionalist conception in favor of the concept of *engaging* which Sewell considers more descriptive of the content of international relations.

When DeGaulle re-inserted nationalism into the integration process, the neo-functionalists were forced to re-examine their premises concerning the influence of economics on politics and to recast their analysis from one describing an inevitability to one describing a possibility. Haas contended not that the exercise was incapable from the start of formulating laws of integration, but that the movement of international relations had made the question of regional integration obsolete.[10] The important question was now not regional integration but that of the global order. Thus, in *Scientists and World Order,* Haas discussed the emergence of an international system remarkably similar to a "functional" world though he does not suggest functionalism as its appropriate name.[11] In an interesting essay in 1982, Haas went beyond all efforts at prediction and suggested that the deepest problem for international relations theory was that it suffered from a division into schools, each of which had its base in a different and opposed epistemology. He suggested that a useful discussion could take place between the schools on the basis of their provisional adoption of an evolutionary epistemology.[12] I have not adopted his epistemology but I would agree that discussion among the schools is in order.

Thompson provides a thorough review of the career and concerns of Niebuhr in his *Masters of International Thought*.[13] Generally speaking, Niebuhr's great concern was the relationship between man and God with history as the intermediary. In general, Thompson's thought has gravitated towards the questions of Christian ethics and realities of power and force in politics (which lend a sense of tragedy to political, social, and personal life).[14] In the case of Niebuhr, functionalism may play a part in some long term development in the relationship between man and God. For Thompson, functionalism seems a possible material means to the ethical goals of peace and social justice.

A number of non-legalist perspectives on integration, world order, and interdependence have emerged since Morgenthau, Sewell, Claude, and Haas first evaluated functionalism.[15] For the most part I have not evaluated Mitrany's functionalism with respect to these perspectives. Whether the re-evaluation of functionalism has a direct bearing on the several approaches depends in great part on the exact discussion by the analyst in question (which I do not wish, for the most part, to prejudge). Nevertheless functionalism does seem to take us into the core of the transformation which many analysts contend is overtaking the state system.

The final chapter examines one organ of the United Nations, the United Nations Environment Programme, from a functionalist perspective. It examines the nature of the problem to which UNEP is addressed, seeks to determine whether UNEP, in its origin, took a practical approach to those problems, and examines the institutional and political framework in which UNEP is set as a partial test of functionalism's potential to help transform the state system into a functional system. I draw no absolute conclusions from the test but do suggest that, as regards the transformation of international relations, UNEP reflects functionalism's potential more than it reflects the success of functionalist process.

NOTES

1. Hans J. Morgenthau, *Politics Among Nations: The Struggle for Power and Peace,* 5th ed. rev. (New York: Alfred Knopf, 1978).
2. See, for example, *In Defense of the National Interest: A Critical Examination of American Foreign Policy* (New York: Alfred Knopf, 1951); *The Purpose of American Politics* (New York: Random House, 1960); and *A New Foreign Policy for the United States* (New York: Praeger, 1969).
3. Hans J. Morgenthau, *Scientific Man Versus Power Politics* (Chicago: University of Chicago Press, 1946).
4. Inis L. Claude, Jr., *Swords Into Plowshares: The Problems and Progress of International Organization,* 4th ed. (New York: Random House, 1971).
5. Inis L. Claude, Jr., *Power and International Relations* (New York: Random House, 1962).
6. Inis L. Claude, Jr., *National Minorities: An International Problem* (New York: Greenwood Press, 1969).
7. Inis L. Claude, Jr., *The Changing United Nations* (New York: Random House, 1967).
8. James P. Sewell, *Functionalism and World Politics: A Study Based on U.N. Programs Financing Economic Development* (Princeton: Princeton University Press, 1966).
9. James P. Sewell, *UNESCO and World Politics: Engaging in International Relations* (Princeton: Princeton University Press, 1975).
10. Ernst B. Haas, *The Obsolescence of Regional Integration Theory* (Berkeley: Institute of International Studies, University of California, 1975).
11. Ernst B. Haas, Mary Pat Williams and Don Babai, *Scientists and World Order: The Use of Technical Knowledge in International Organizations* (Berkeley: University of California Press, 1977).
12. Ernst B. Haas, "Words Can Hurt You: Or Who Said What, to Whom, About Regimes," *International Organization,* Vol. 36, No. 2 (Spring 1982), pp. 207–243.
13. Kenneth W. Thompson, *Masters of International Thought: Major Twentieth Century Theorists and the World Crisis* (Baton Rouge: Louisiana State University Press, 1980).
14. See Kenneth W. Thompson, *Understanding World Politics* (Notre Dame: University of Notre Dame Press, 1975); *Ethics, Functionalism, and Power in International Politics* (Baton Rouge: Louisiana State University Press, 1979); *The Moral Issue in Statecraft: Twentieth Century Approaches and Problems* (Baton Rouge: Louisiana State University Press, 1966); and *Foreign Assistance: A View From the Private Sector* (Notre Dame: University of Notre Dame Press, 1972).

15. Though a bit dated, Richard Falk provides a good review of the general approaches currently taken toward the study of interdependence and world order in "Contending Approaches to World Order," *Journal of International Affairs,* Vol. 31, No. 2 (Fall/Winter 1977), pp. 171–198. With respect to integration studies, Ernst Haas, "The Study of Regional Integration: Reflections on the Joy and Anguish of Pre-Theorizing," *International Organization,* Vol. 24, No. 4 (Autumn 1970), pp. 607–646, provides a good review of the successes and problems of the study of integration. Though it is hardly complete the bibliography in this work cites sources from several of the approaches. Though not incorporated into the body of this work, many of them were used as a check against unfortunate turns in the development of this study.

CHAPTER ONE

David Mitrany and Functionalism

The implications of modern international organization in the humanitarian, economic, and social fields are expressed in a thoughtful way by the argument for functionalism. But, by speaking of a thoughtful *argument* we also acknowledge the possibility that these forms of international organization require no thought beyond that which underpins the national state system of the twentieth century. These organizations may exist solely for the sake of, and as appendages of, the national state.[1] If this, in fact, were the case, one might wish to monitor from time to time the administration of these agencies. One would not, however, look to these agencies as either the source of, or reflection of "system transformations."[2] There is, however, an eclectic body of thought which is held together by the view that international politics, and therefore, all politics, are in the process of an essential transformation. To the extent that one wishes to investigate this view, functionalism offers both a thoughtful analysis of the sources of this possible transformation and a persuasive rationale for the contention that international organization and transnational[3] activity create and reflect the gradual emergence of a new type of political organization which lies "beyond the nation-state."[4] _HAAS

Since the term functionalism has lent its authority to more than one body of social thought[5] it should be made clear at this early stage that the functionalism to which we refer is that most closely associated with the work of David Mitrany. The basic propositions of this thought are considered by Mitrany to be both empirical and normative. Its initial contention is that social and economic coop-

1

source of war?

eration between states will (and should) erode the "ubiquitous" yet "anachronistic" place held by territorial states in the modern world.[6] Its corollary is that the result of this erosion will be (and should be) a more peaceful world.[7]

Mitrany, of course, was not the sole expositor of this line of thought. However, not only is his the name most closely associated with this brand of functionalism, but his thought also expresses functionalism in a cohesive manner (for which reason those who have explored functionalism invariably cite his work as expressing the core of the doctrine). Some writers have suggested that Mitrany is and should be considered an independent political thinker, responsible for a new approach to political things.[8] Without prejudging the claim, the work which follows proceeds on the possibility of that claim. In order to examine the argument of functionalism we will examine critically the major works of David Mitrany.

The most influential of Mitrany's essays was *A Working Peace System*.[9] Though the most widely read, *A Working Peace System* is not the most comprehensive account of functionalism. It, along with other essays and monographs which he published, is a helpful complement for the study of Mitrany's work. The most useful sources for insight into functionalism are his work, compiled from the Dodge lectures at Yale, entitled *The Progress of International Government*[10] and the collected observations in *The Functional Theory of Politics*.[11] *The Progress of International Government* set forth and elaborated Mitrany's functional idea. We will endeavor both to highlight the thrust of Mitrany's general argument and to investigate, by way of reference to *The Progress of International Government* and Mitrany's other works, the argument in greater depth.

We may discern the thrust of Mitrany's work by pointing to an observation which he makes in the Introduction to *The Progress of International Government*. Mitrany notes that the Greeks, working by intuition, discovered and elaborated the truth "that the limits and functions of authority, the rights and duties of citizenship have in their core some eternal relationship to human nature, no matter what the size and shape of a particular society."[12] The Greeks' intuition concerning politics was, according to Mitrany, so powerful that even today their authority approaches "finality."[13] *The Progress of International Government* is not, of course, a commentary on Greek political philosophy; the most it does is to

recommend that thought to the interested student. However, Mitrany
does derive one dictum from his reading of Aristotle. That is that,
" . . . the permanent end of any political community is to make its
members happy."[14] The problem which Mitrany addresses in the
rest of the lecture and, for that matter, in the greater part of his
writings is how this end may be achieved in the modern world.

According to Mitrany it is a mistake to equate the political
community with the modern national state. The state is one form
of political community but by no means the only possible form.
Historically, the national state merely replaced a feudal-ecclesiastical
form of political organization (which itself replaced the Roman
Imperium). That is to say, man may have an eternal relation to
political rights and duties but the form of the community to which
these rights and duties are related neither need be, nor historically
has been, eternal. Since there is nothing eternal about the national
state it is fair to subject not only the character of domestic regimes
to criticism (as was done by political scientists of an earlier day)
but also the state system itself. Conveniently, the standard by
which this system can be judged is the same as that proposed by
Aristotle, namely, whether it achieves its final end of making the
individuals within the system happy. Within reasonable limits, a
transition to a new form of political community is defensible and
desirable if the state system cannot meet its objective.[15]

Mitrany's position is that the modern national state has ceased
to serve the permanent end of political communities. Not only
does the state fail to make its members happy, but the system of
states has " . . . reached a point where the material forces at our
disposal threaten to escape our control and to warp the very
civilization which they were meant to enhance."[16] In short, whatever its value in meeting the needs of previous generations, the era
when the nation-state served as a useful agent to political community and human happiness has passed. To the extent that this is the
case the international system is faced with a crisis.

Functionalism is, in a sense, Mitrany's solution to the crisis
facing the state system. A brief explanation is necessary here,
however, for Mitrany did not see functionalism so much as the
solution to the crisis as a way of looking at that crisis. To the extent
that functionalism is the cure for the disease it lies in pointing
political people to the right questions and a reasonable analysis of
the problem. The basic question is, again, that of the happiness of

functionalism - human activity in to various purposes
separation
of

the members of the political community. To Mitrany, such an approach will be reflected institutionally by a devaluation of the state, whose organization traditionally governed specific territorial entities and, in some cases, specific ethnic groupings, in favor of organized activities tailored to perform observable and specific functions necessary to the well-being of the members of the political community. The scope of these functions is limited internally by the specificity of their various objectives and externally or instrumentally by their contribution to the overriding end of political communities. At the heart of Mitrany's political project is the conviction that territorial political organization should be replaced by functional political organization. At the heart of that conviction lies an analysis which separates human activities into the various purposes for which they are undertaken, and in turn relates these purposes to, and treats them as aspects of, the larger goal of human happiness.

This brief overview of Mitrany's functionalism should be supplemented by two subsidiary points. The first point raises the problem of history. Mitrany's view of the world is progressive. Without delving too deeply into the problem at this stage we may illustrate the point by reference to Mitrany's perception of the history of the modern world. From the time of Machiavelli to the 19th century, Europe progressed from autocratic and theocratic politics to the politics of democratic individualism within nation-states. From the 19th century to date politics within nation-states has been undergoing another progression from democratic individualism to democratic communitarianism. Secondly, while the progress of politics has not been entirely peaceful the time when fundamental change could be assisted by violence is past. It is now necessary, and to that extent possible, that the progress toward new political configurations be peaceful.[17]

Because of this emphasis on the necessity for a peaceful evolution toward a new political system it is easy to abstract Mitrany's "solution" from his analysis of the problem. This is not wrong but it does tend to limit the scope of inquiry within bounds too narrow for Mitrany's work. For example, James P. Sewell has characterized functionalism as the contention that "the most desirable route to international community-building proceeds gradually from initial trans-national cooperation in the solution of common problems."[18] This is an adequate description of the functional process but, in so characterizing functionalism, one makes functionalism appear as simply a method or a tool for international community builders, even if they use the tool haphazardly or without thinking "functionalism." It is also a key to a broad approach to the understanding of politics. It is this approach itself which I wish to examine as I expand and develop the short synopsis of functionalism presented above.

I
FUNCTIONALISM AND THE STATE

We may begin our examination of Mitrany's thought by taking up the most obvious aspect of that thought: his depreciation of the state. We may then pass through his understanding of the state and its obsolescence to his understanding of the task of political science in the twentieth century (which from his perspective is an historic task).

Mitrany's discussion of the state is somewhat superficial (by self-description) in *The Progress of International Government*. The state, as Mitrany summarized it, is a creation of and within history. Thus the state emerged out of the Renaissance and Reformation as a theoretical and practical claim of theoreticians and princes to temporal power and authority, and power of the Roman Church. The works of Machiavelli and Bodin justified this claim politically, Luther and the other reformers justified this claim theologically, and princes instituted the claim practically. The essence of this claim was political individuality. This claim, or at least the period which produced it, marked for Mitrany "one of those rare metabolic shifts in human outlook."[19]

The principle of equality both emerged with and formed an essential part of the claim to individuality on the part of, and on behalf of, princes. The work of Grotius exemplified this point clearly by formulating the juridical principle of state equality through which the prince or state is legitimated in acting as its own judge in a dispute. As principles, then, individuality and equality emerged as two sides of the same coin. The legitimation of individual activity undertaken without the sanction of the universal authority of the Pope required that the prince be seen as the equal of the

Pope in the temporal realm, and that the Pope's spiritual authority
be divested of its capacity to constrain political authority. The
possibility of individualism depended on the possibility of, or
principle of, equality.[20]

The principles of individualism and equality emerged as the
practical right of princes to act independently of higher authority
in political matters. Yet the history of the principles did not end
with the establishment of the state, or more properly, the princely
state. With respect to formal relations between states, the principles did define a "static" relationship. However, within the states,
the principles undermined the legitimacy of princes themselves in
favor of democratic individualism. Thus from the Renaissance/
Reformation until the 19th century the process of state building
was essentially an internal process. The practical process involved
the creation of the constitutional state in which individuals were
guaranteed first equality or individuality before the law, followed
later by equality or individuality in the formulation of the law itself
or, in other words, first legal equality and then political equality.[21]

The effect of the introduction of individualism, and the constitutionalism which protected the individual, into politics was not,
however, to enshrine that principle for all time. Rather, the idea of
equality which emerged out of individualism really defined the
progress of the age. Once the common man was permitted into
political councils it was only a matter of time before he used that
political right to turn the state, now understood as the sum of equal
individual wills, into an instrument for his use rather than regarding the state simply as the source of tyranny (which it had been in
fact while autocracy and aristocracy ruled). The emergence of the
welfare state corresponded precisely with, and was a practical
result of, the positive use by the mass of their newly granted
political power. Since the end of the state was now properly
identified with the end of the majority of its citizens, the state
legitimately turned its powers to the support of the demand for
social welfare or social justice. While social welfare need not mean
precise social or economic equality, it did mean that certain opportunities would be made available to all citizens. Thus the welfare
state represents the natural end of state building, and the community has re-established itself on the basis of the intrinsic justice of
legal, political and social equality.[22]

The modern state cannot, however, be understood on the basis of strictly legal, political, and social relations between abstract individuals. Communitarian politics is a natural result of the democratic revolution; nationalism is the final political result of this democratic/communitarian revolution as it interacts with ethnicity. In as much as the notion of political equality grants to each individual the right to a voice in the determination of his political fate, it is understandable that he should choose to share that fate with members of his own ethnic group. The national state which results represents an organic relationship beyond the simply organization of welfare activities which the state does for a majority in any community. In the modern era the national state thus serves both the material needs (social welfare) and the spiritual needs (ethnic home) of people. (In this sense for Mitrany the "biological" ground of ethnicity apparently develops into and is represented by the "spirit" of ethnicity or nationalism). Thus modern political life is the national, communitarian/egalitarian, welfare state.[23]

We would be remiss if we did not also point to a third aspect of the egalitarian revolution. This aspect may appropriately be termed the economic aspect. We hesitate to separate economics from politics in Mitrany's thought because the development of political communitarianism (though not nationalism) is intricately connected in Mitrany's thought to the development of economic life. The point to be made in the first instance is that, in conjunction with state-building in its constitutional/individualist phase, the economic character of the world changed. The techniques necessary to control man's economic fate emerged under *laissez faire,* yet they seem to Mitrany to have been only the initial stages of man's effort to control material existence. The control of material existence is the theme not only of economics but also of science, which therefore is coextensive with modern economy. State involvement in science and economics may be said to represent the effect of the communitarian ethos on this activity. Thus a project to control material existence begun by individuals in one era was, in keeping with the communitarian transformation, made a community project in the next.[24]

It is far from Mitrany's purpose to argue with the past development of political, legal, and social/economic life in the modern era. At least in terms of strictly municipal political development this process has been a positive one. The development of the modern national welfare state out of the feudal/ecclesiastical autocratic past was a lengthy, sometimes violent, but worthwhile process. Yet, that development has created a new task for both thought and practice. The state has now become a self-contradiction. If the modern welfare state gains its reason for being from the end which it serves (that is, the happiness of its citizens) its purpose is now undermined by the physical impossibility of fulfilling that purpose. It is impossible for the state to fulfill its purpose primarily because of the economic/scientific developments of the last several centuries, which can both lead and reflect the material demands or expectations of the citizens of the welfare state.[25]

Let us summarize this point. Within the confines of some constitutional framework, the mass-democratic welfare state exists out of consideration for and by the approval of its members, meaning that the conditions of their happiness is its primary responsibility. The conditions which the state must secure if its citizens are to be happy are legal equality, political equality, and if not precise social/economic equality at least some semblance of it (by which we may understand sufficient and equal access to those physical goods of society which are at least a necessary part of human happiness). In order to aid its citizens the state takes over the duty to regulate the economy both for the sake of stability and for the sake of growth. The contradiction or crisis of the modern state emerges at the points where first, the state can no longer control economic processes vital to the material well-being of the state (inasmuch as labor, production, and distribution are differentiated both within and between states); secondly, the scientific advances of the modern era have introduced opportunities for travel and communication which are virtually universal; and thirdly, services made possible by science—disease control, weather prediction, etc.—can only be offered on the basis of knowledge obtained from, and applied to, geographic areas beyond state boundaries.[26] This condition is, of course, the same as we commonly recognize when we speak of interdependence. (We may add in passing that warfare has been equally universalized in its range of destructiveness). Thus, just at the point where it became the state's responsibility to protect and aid its citizens by positive action and regulation, or, put in more Mitranian terms, just as the state assumed the responsibility to meet the needs (demands) of its citizens, it found itself in a situation where the job could not be done by the state acting independently.[27] As already quoted, we have " . . . reached a point where the material forces at our disposal threaten to escape our control and to warp the very civilization which they were meant to enhance."[28]

The development of universal or near universal scientific/ economic society means that for decisive purposes the state is obsolete. Were recognition of this condition coextensive with the condition Mitrany would see no crisis. However, for the most part neither the citizens nor the leaders of modern states recognize the essential obsolescence of the state. The source of this failed perception seems to be the current fusion of material and spiritual functions which the state now represents. The state as the current abode of national feeling accentuates and warps the natural spiritual life of a people.[29] Yet it is precisely this accentuation of the spiritual life of a people into nationalism that permits the state to interfere with the effective organization of their material life.[30] Nothing shows this more clearly according to Mitrany than the failure of the European system during the period between the two World Wars. At the point where broader forms of economic activity were called for, the European state system embraced more firmly the principle of economic autarky. It did this, not because economies would function more effectively, but because of the warped spiritual pretentions of nationalism.[31]

According to Mitrany, a functional analysis of the self-contradiction of the state shows that, in its effort to stabilize the economy, and to foster economic and scientific progress, the state as it currently exists is bound to fail. Economic and scientific activities are limited not by territorial boundaries but by their very purposes themselves. Some of these functions, in fact, require a universal scale if they are to be performed adequately. On the other hand the spiritual life of a people is limited to the range of that people (admittedly) but there is nothing sacrosanct in state representation of cultural or spiritual life. Therefore a sound functional analysis exposes the failure of the state at the same time that it recommends or shows the way to overcome or deal with the crisis. What is necessary, if a catastrophe is to be avoided, is that the spiritual life of people be decoupled from their material life. That is, the solution to the crisis of the state in the 20th century is that the state "wither away" or at the very least be significantly devalued.[32]

To state the argument in another way, the decoupling of spirit-

ual life and material life may be accomplished by a simple commitment on the part of present leaders and citizens to finding solutions
to the numerous material problems which beset their polities.
Immediately upon assuming the commitment to solve problems,
form follows function. Since each material function sets its own
standards of performance, there is of course no *set* form, though
an outline of functional organization can be suggested. Where the
state is either too large or too small to perform the economic/
scientific functions effectively, they can be turned over to private
or public agencies whose size and structure will be determined by
the needs of the function itself. Since, for the most part, these will
be technical/bureaucratic types of activities these agencies will be
staffed primarily by experts.[33] In Mitranian terms the question as
to the public or private nature of these agencies is somewhat
ill-formed. In fact, if there still remains an important theoretical
question, as opposed to the practical task at hand of separating the
spiritual from the material in social organization, it is the confused
but related problem of the meaning of the public and the private.
The task of moving into the functional world needs for its success a
fundamental rethinking of the public and private realms in human
life.[34] But he elsewhere suggests that practicality or function can
solve this problem as well, for the question becomes primarily one
of efficiency.

The benefits of the functional approach will come in three
major areas. First, people's material lives will improve because the
artificial boundaries of states will no longer interfere with economic and scientific activity. Secondly, the spiritual life of people
will take on a more normal tenor and, in fact, be permitted to
flourish as a true individual and cultural life because it will no
longer be restrained and warped by the straitjacket of the state.
Finally, material and spiritual life will prosper jointly by the potential elimination of the greatest problem caused by their fusion, that
being the problem of warfare (particularly considering the devasta-
tion and emotional abandon of modern international conflict).

Since functionalism is both an analysis of a problem and a
program of action, Mitrany considered the possible success, and
the means of instituting his program. The world cannot pass from a
system of nation-states to a functional world overnight. While
people can perhaps perceive over time that the material benefits
which they derive from the state may be better attained by other

means, they will not readily agree to a wholesale transfer of authority and functions to new entities. Nor, given the considerable hold which nationalism has on people, are they likely to change suddenly their emotional attachment to the state. In addition to the educational problem of reorienting the life of the spirit away from its fulfillment in the state there remains a problem of trust in the future under such an arrangement. People are raised to consider other states as either hostile or potentially hostile. It is difficult for them to imagine working harmoniously with other peoples without the prospect of addressing major differences between them by resorting to force. Mitrany suggests that the barriers which separate people may be dismantled gradually. That is, the broader aim of separating spiritual life from material life on a universal basis can be accomplished by the gradual institution of international activities which perform cooperative, functional tasks. This will not, in the short term, do away with traditional politics, understood as balance of power politics, nor will it do away with all conflict in the new system. It will start people down the road to a form of material cooperation which can, over time, "bring them actively together" rather than simply trying to keep them peacefully apart.[35]

As a philosophical contention, Mitrany states that there are no longer absolute questions remaining to be answered. There are only the practical questions of how people may best order their lives for the greatest mutual benefit. We are basically beyond the great philosophical questions, which have been answered, and have merely pragmatic life to get on with.[36] Mitrany is never very clear about why the great philosophical questions are solved. In one sense he suggests that the theoretical and political establishment of communitarian legal, political and social equality leave no more questions to be asked. The meaning of life and death as a question has been in part answered because a man's life is a part of a continuous community life and in the other part answered because personal salvation (to the extent that that salvation is distinct from community life) is an individual not a political affair. In another sense, however, he indicates that these questions are only solved for the age and that in another age there will be different solutions. In a final sense economic necessity could be said to drive both alternatives. The permanence of the solution to the problem of scarcity conditions, perhaps, the answer to the meaning of life and death.

The state is no longer a positive horizon for man, but a restriction, or negative limit, on his possibilities—both spiritual and material. It is, therefore, an anachronism. The same may be said for rigid adherence either to a particular form of political organization or to particular political ideologies. Ideologies and rigid political forms (constitutions) only interfere with the "task at hand"—if they do not positively impose evil on the world. Rigid constitutionalism hindered the USA from responding quickly to the crisis of the Great Depression.[37] An even more perverse adherence by European socialists to the Marxian doctrine of the citification of the countryside kept them from forming an alliance with the Peasant parties of eastern Europe (a wholly logical proposition since both parties were basically "workingman's parties.") Instead the Communists found a tactical wedge into power which permitted them to impose an even more destructive and violent adherence to abstract and archaic principle in the collectivization drives.[38]

This is spiritually and materially a communitarian age. The progress of democracy and economy went beyond the individualism which held sway into the twentieth century. The communitarian age had been elaborated in thought for and accepted practically by the peoples of nearly every state in the world. While this set of circumstances still requires that a new understanding of the public and private be worked out, this is not for Mitrany a purely theoretical question, but a question of sound practice. Progressive activity has finished with the merely abstract. It concentrates on solving problems as they emerge on the scene. This inevitably and justifiably involves planning. This, broadly stated, is the functional project. We now turn to the understanding of politics in which it is grounded.

II
FUNCTIONALISM AND POLITICS

"Modern political theory," says Mitrany, "has sought to identify and sift the elements of power: between the state's authority and particular institutions (the estates, the church, etc.) and individuals; and within the state's authority itself, the distribution of power between the crown and parliament and executive. In a general and varying way there was a public 'political' sphere and a 'non-political' sphere, private and institutional. All these divisions and distinctions now are being steadily overlaid."[39] The modern project, until the 20th century, aimed to separate and fix various levels of authority and spheres of competence. However, near the core of that project lay a distinction between state and society which no longer applies. As Mitrany explains, "What it amounts to is that the grand distinction between state and society upon which all modern political theory rested is vanishing rapidly. In most sectors of life the public and the private are flowing into each other without any set or clear bounds."[40] Politics is therefore undergoing, or is in the process of completing, a basic transformation in content.

Let us examine this transformation briefly. In the 19th century the content of "politics" was considered to be what was done by government. Yet, under the influence of individualism what the government was permitted to do was severely circumscribed by the private sector. In the 20th century all that has changed; as Mitrany says, all the distinctions between public and private have broken down. Most human life is now political, or public, life. Nothing more clearly points out this fact than the advent of the welfare state, for it represents the fusion of economics (which had been considered a private affair in the 19th century) and governance. "When the state assumes such vast functions it must attract to itself the means and powers for their performance. In constitutional terms one might put the problem this way: that popular government was brought about to fence in the power of the state, now it calls it forth on the widest possible scale."[41] This is not accidental but in the very nature of the democratic revolution. Mitrany concludes that, "One cannot have only one side of the coin. And the paradoxical meaning for our enquiry is that whenever public authority in a state, whether unitary or federal, takes charge of any sector of social and economic life, political theory in the traditional sense has nothing more to say."[42] Thus, social life whether public or private is increasingly becoming pragmatic.

The meaning of this pragmatism is not that conflict will disappear, but that pragmatism can be a means of peaceful change. As Mitrany says, "A society is marked more by that ability to dissolve conflict than by the provisions for juridical surgery. Conflicts between various *interests* are not fought out with arms precisely because they are part of a complex of social relationships. The grounds and ends of conflict are usually concrete and specific; hence they can be identified as a particular 'case' capable of being examined and settled as such."[43] While it may be true that all life is now, in a sense, political and practical, Mitrany still sees at work in the world two types of politics: one type dissolves conflict and the other exacerbates conflicts out of a rigid adherence to fixed political forms or ideologies. The latter type of politics is most noticeable on the international scene and manifests itself as power politics. He contrasts this type of politics to the notion of service or more accurately, service politics, which has become the norm of modern democratic politics. He does not say that pragmatic politics dispenses with power. Rather he distinguishes between the "ends" of power.[44]

Pragmatic or service politics can be reduced to: first, administration and, secondly, the dissolution of conflict by peaceful means.[45] International relations manifests itself as power politics because states are rigid forms often governed through use of ideologies. Once the state begins to recede in importance, politics can and will take on the image of managing social relations rather than of a contest for power.

Functional politics does not ignore the fact that there will always be bureaucratic politics and social cleavages. Functional politics does however maintain that if the source of these cleavages is discovered a peaceful solution can be found. In functional politics a rational solution to the problem of bureaucratic politics[46] is also possible because, if taken seriously, functions impose their own limit. Finally functional/pragmatic/service politics deals with questions of economics and science, that is with material life. The economic/scientific revolution, having outpaced the capacity of states to control its consequences, can be brought under control or at least directed only by a politics suited to the dynamic of science and economics. The essential feature of economics and science and technology is change. In fact, if it were not the case before, it is true now that the fundamental condition of life, if we may speak of it as a condition, is change. Therefore politics or social life cannot be packaged any longer into neat constitutional arrangements nor can ideology lead or direct social life—at least a "set" ideology, as opposed to a "way" of thinking.[47]

The global issues which have emerged as a result of advances in economy and science (pollution, transportation, communication) mean territoriality no longer has a content. To the extent that government is the sum of its functions, modern government or politics is becoming less of a government every day because it can no longer perform its functions. For practical purposes all human life increasingly takes on the appearance of public life but the modern public sector—the state—has less and less ability to support that public life.

Mitrany says,

> That we are going through a crisis in political outlook is evident: one cannot put it down to a decline in political fervor, like the decline in religion, for the surge towards the 'good society' and so the wrestling with politics is more than ever with us. Rather the crisis is one of political confusion . . . confusion from trying to work an epochal change in social direction with the outworn ways and forms of the individualist-nationalist period.
>
> It took centuries to wean society away from human sacrifices on the altar of the gods, only to see it replaced with the sacrificial altar of the state; and while at times people have rebelled against the individual authority of gods and kings, they cannot rebel against their own all-providing collective deity. It is beyond us who live in the turmoil of the transition to grasp how great a historical turning point ours may prove to be; we stand at a cross-roads, but do not know what kind of world we are reaching for. In some fundamental ways we are breaking out of the earthbound history of man, as it has been since its beginning, and moving into a new universe of action and relationships.[48]

What Mitrany tells us above points out another feature of his conception of politics: that history is the mediator between thought and politics. History, Mitrany suggests, marches onward. The individualistic 19th century has inevitably and irretrievably given way to the communal 20th century, and politics must adjust to the march of history, even as it enters a new universe. The fusion of spiritual life and economic life was the zenith of the state but also its gravest defect and the politics of the future must be careful to separate the two. That is, spiritual life should be left to culture, while material life should be dissected by function and re-established on the basis of the intrinsic scope of the particular functions. A precise picture of the new universe is not available but the functional process can and will permit an alignment of the historical demands of people and technology with the practical possibility of meeting those demands. In short, history has created mass democratic politics and destroyed the meaning of the old principled distinction between public and private. Since all politics at the national level is now democratic it is also pragmatic. As actors in history we have the task of breaking down the walls of the nation-states so that that pragmatic approach to living together informs not only domestic society but global society. History is the source of· this task, the source, that is, of an historically changing set of functional problems and their solutions, and the new tasks lead us forward into history.

Finally, Mitrany tells us that once nationality and economic activity are handled by means other than, or in addition to, the national state the security function will be seen in its true light. Mitrany discusses the issues of security and international law quite extensively in his work. He never advocates simple disarmament and he invariably lends verbal support to efforts designed to share the security function among states. He points out that since enforcement of the law (international law) was left to individual states, they had no means except their own force for dealing with recalcitrant parties.[49] He also notes that the 20th century has seen an effort to transfer the right of individual states to make war to the "collective society of nations."[50] Yet the sanctions available to that collective society:

> will in the end be determined by the jurisdiction of any new international authority; and as one might expect in a world composed of sovereign states, the wider that jurisdiction the smaller the need for stringent instruments of execution. The renunciation of national force in no way would imply a corresponding increase in international force, but quite the contrary, when the nations will feel themselves to be part of a world commonwealth, sanctions will become as much an anachronism as they would be at present in the United States, where the individual states no longer think in terms of self defense among themselves.[51]

Nationalist and ideological competition draw states back to the original international law of self-enforcement. Legal schemes or federal schemes for dealing with war, and sanctions without a corresponding community are so many words. Mitrany is not against the development and growth of international law—particularly of the administrative type. But his general view is that law must reflect social reality and that community law requires international community. International community is created by common needs and activities. In a democratic, technological age the real sanction for government is the non-satisfaction of citizen needs. If the social revolution of which he speaks is as fundamental as he maintains, democratic demands will eventually constrain governments to more and more compliance with international norms. Security will at that point be merely a function, not the fundamental fact of international relations.

III
FUNCTIONALISM AND POLITICAL SCIENCE

The functionalist conception of political science emerges out of Mitrany's conception of history. Mitrany says that the task of the political scientist is not to predict but rather, following Hobhouse, to make clear the "relation of things."[52] Political science, says Mitrany, "works on the assumption that there is an inescapable causal relationship between communal ends and political means."[53] The things which are discussed in the case of political science may be understood to be human beings, their doings and their material surroundings.

Mitrany's political science, or analysis of the "relation of things", indicates that, given the ends of human action, some means are suited to achieving those ends, while others are not. For example, if the primary end of communal existence is happiness understood as material satisfaction achieved by way of public services, that existence can no longer be circumscribed by territorial boundaries, but rests on the type of means and activities which the services themselves call forth. Functionalism does not seek to predict events in any precise manner, nor does it seek to lay bare the decision-making process (inasmuch as the process itself is inevitably colored by the task at hand). Functionalism stakes its claim on seeing the real world and in not encapsulating that world in abstraction. In other words,

> Functionalism knows only one logic, the logic of the problem, and of a problem apt to be always in flux in its elements, its spread and its effects. Functionalism is never still, but it attaches to society the things that brought it there; and to be true to its social purpose it must implicitly be self-adjusting. At no point of action are conditions exactly as they were before or likely to be later; and at no point of action are the policymakers likely to know all the facts or foresee all the effects of their decisions. Natural science also is vitally concerned with change but 'as development, as evolution, as unfolding. If nature is forever flux, it is for all that, functional and self-sustaining.'[54]

To attack the problems then is to dissect social life with the same objectivity and sensitivity to flux as the natural scientist brings to his study of nature.

We are left to conclude then that the difference between functional science and natural science is no more than the difference between human beings and nature. Just as we have no specific way of knowing what directions evolution will take with respect to species (though in fact we can approximate closely the course of elementary matter) we have no way of knowing *precisely* what the future will be, for the needs of democratic society evolve in ways not dissimilar to the ways of nature. In spite of this the steps we take to resolve a problem are, in a way, experiments to be refined as we have greater or lesser success with the approach.[55] The method of functionalism is then to break the human activities and problems into their parts. As Mitrany says, "Everybody feels a sentiment of humanity but few act naturally upon it, because action has to be linked to concrete steps within the range of everyday life."[56] In short, Mitrany's political science rests on the inescapable link between communal ends and political means.

The tasks of political scientists are to search out those areas of common concern and to educate people into functional modes of thought. "The heart and mind of man are malleable, and the genius of each period has known that it requires but good will and patience to give them the sight of progress."[57] Political science, says Mitrany, must become "an instrument devoted . . . to the service of human progress."[58]

International organizations, both governmental and nongovernmental, are the primary means of international cooperative activities. NGO's, in their contact with IGO's, informal or formal (such as in the ILO), create a marriage of technical control and popular participation. This technical democracy is a process which can and should be encouraged, and it is the purpose of political science to do so. Techniques of management can be left to experts but the humanism of genuine political science, its concern for the welfare of all, puts it in the service of progress. That purpose is best served by a continuous concern for function.

NOTES

1. It is of course true that many of the states in the interstate system are not national states, at least in terms of the general understanding of nationality. An elementary, yet useful, distinction between the nation and the state may be found in Theodore Couloumbis and James Wolfe, *An Introduction to International Relations: Power and Justice* (Englewood Cliffs: Prentice-Hall, 1982), Chapter 4. For a considerably more sophisticated discussion of the problems posed for interstate relations by the multinational state see Inis L. Claude, Jr., *National Minorities*. Many others might be cited but to no advantage. Since the beginning of the Nineteenth Century the union of state and nation has been the ideal type of political organization.
2. The notion of system transformation is also prevalent in the literature. See for instance Ernst Haas, *Beyond the Nation-State* (Stanford: Stanford University Press, 1964), p. 77.
3. Robert O. Keohane and Joseph S. Nye, Jr., eds. *Transnational Relations and World Politics* (Cambridge: Harvard University Press, 1971). Picking up on Raymond Aron's distinction between the state system and the transnational society which contains it, Keohane and Nye argued that transnational interactions promote attitude changes and international pluralism, create dependence and interdependence as well as new instruments for influence, and with the existence of autonomous transnational organizations, aggravate or ameliorate conditions between states. On the basis of these conclusions the authors argue for a new understanding of politics and particularly world politics. They would move away from the "state-centric" understanding of world politics toward a definition which sees politics "as all

political interactions between significant actors in a world system in which a significant actor is any somewhat autonomous individual or organization that controls substantial resources and participates in political relations with other actors across state lines," pp. xxii–xxv.

4. Haas, *Beyond the Nation-State.*

5. Gabriel A. Almond and G. Bingham Powell, Jr., *Comparative Politics: A Developmental Approach.* In Sociology see Talcott Parsons, *The Social System.* These are two sources of functionalism and structural functionalism. In general the notion of functions was taken from anthropology and sociology and applied to political systems. We feel under no necessity to trace the origin and meaning of other forms of functionalism as our interest is in one particular brand. Also, see Paul Taylor and A. J. R. Groom, *International Organization: A Conceptual Approach* (New York: Nichols Publishing Co., 1978), p. 236.

6. David Mitrany, *The Functional Theory of Politics* (London: Martin Robertson, 1975), p. 256. Also, see *A Working Peace System* (Chicago: Quadrangle Books, 1966), p. 150.

7. Mitrany, *The Progress of International Government* (New Haven: Yale University Press, 1932), pp. 118–130. For example, see *A Working Peace System,* p. 15, "A true international society would begin to take shape when a general concern for social security would begin to loom larger than the concern for military security."

8. Mitrany, *Progress, Functional Theory of Politics;* Haas, *Beyond the Nation-State;* Claude, *Swords Into Plowshares;* Morgenthau, *Politics Among Nations,* pp. 525–529; Thompson, *Ethics, Functionalism, and Power in International Politics,* p. 61; Paul Taylor and A. J. R. Groom, eds. *International Organization: A Conceptual Approach* (London: Frances Pinter, Ltd. and New York: Nichols Publishing Co., 1978), *Functionalism: Theory and Practice in International Relations* (New York: Crane, Russak Co., 1975).

9. Mitrany, *A Working Peace System.*

10. Mitrany, *The Progress of International Government* (hereafter referred to as *P.I.G.*).

11. Mitrany, *The Functional Theory of Politics* (hereafter referred to as *F.T.P.*).

12. Mitrany, *P.I.G.,* p. 16.

13. Ibid.

14. Ibid., p. 17. Whether this precisely describes Aristotle's thought is questionable. For Aristotle happiness is the end of human life and the fulfillment of that end requires politics. It is possible to find in Aristotle a place where he says that the end of politics is the happiness of most citizens but he ties this happiness to the virtue of the

citizens. See Aristotle, *Politics,* trans. Rackham (Cambridge: Harvard University Press, 1972), pp. 213–216.

15. Ibid., pp. 16–52.
16. Ibid., p. 17.
17. Ibid., pp. 16–52. See also Mitrany, *A Working Peace System,* p. 20 and *F.T.P.,* p. 242.
18. Sewell, *Functionalism and World Politics.*
19. Mitrany, *P.I.G.,* p. 24.
20. Ibid., pp. 25–31. See also Mitrany, *A Working Peace System,* p. 20.
21. Ibid., pp. 31–36.
22. Ibid., pp. 37–52.
23. Ibid., pp. 340–341. See also Mitrany, *F.T.P.,* p. 34.
24. Ibid., pp. 97–102. See also Mitrany, *F.T.P.,* pp. 243–245, 266 and 267.
25. Ibid.
26. Mitrany, *F.T.P.,* pp. 243, 244, 249, 250–252.
27. Ibid., p. 243.
28. Mitrany, *P.I.G.,* p. 17.
29. Ibid., pp. 131–134, 136–137. See also Mitrany, *F.T.P.,* pp. 35, 137–145.
30. Ibid. See also Mitrany, *A Working Peace System,* p. 151 and *F.T.P.,* pp. 137–145.
31. Mitrany, *F.T.P.,* pp. 172, 206–207. See also Mitrany, *P.I.G.,* pp. 120–121.
32. Mitrany, *P.I.G.,* p. 98: "But it is no less possible that we may come to the contrary conclusion, and decide that in its present form the State is rather an obstacle in the path of our civilized ideals. No one can be certain that our needs demand that we should discard the State altogether, in the Marxian or anarchist sense." See also p. 134: "The national state has had to coax them (the nations) into some measure of uniformity in the service of its own ends. It was but the continuation of the policy which the State had pursued with regard to religious belief, as long as a unitary church was one of its foundations. Separation of religious belief from political allegiance was one way to freedom of conscience, removing from the jurisdiction of the State a function for which it was clearly unfit. In much the same way only the separation of cultural life from political allegiance will lead to genuine cultural freedom, allowing, as with religious belief, subdivisions within the state and links with kindred groups beyond the state." In addition, see Mitrany, *A Working Peace System,* p. 99: "The functional way may seem a spiritless solution-and so it is, in the sense that it detaches from the spirit the things which are of the body . . . the things which are truly of the spirit—and therefore personal to the individual and to the nation—will not be less winged for being freed in their time from that worldly ballast."
33. Mitrany, *A Working Peace System,* pp. 121–128.

34. Mitrany, *F.T.P.,* pp. 244, 246–247.
35. Mitrany, *A Working Peace System,* pp. 62, 64, 67, 92.
36. Mitrany, *F.T.P.,* pp. 246–247.
37. Ibid., pp. 160–163.
38. This provides the general theme of Mitrany's interesting book, *Marx Against the Peasant.*
39. Mitrany, *F.T.P.,* p. 245.
40. Ibid., p. 246.
41. Ibid.
42. Ibid., p. 247.
43. Ibid., p. 253.
44. Ibid., pp. 246, 251–154.
45. Ibid., pp. 252–255.
46. Ibid., pp. 250, 256–257, 261.
47. Ibid., p. 256.
48. Ibid., pp. 263–264.
49. Mitrany, *P.I.G.,* p. 145.
50. Ibid., p. 147.
51. Ibid., p. 171.
52. Ibid., pp. 64–65 (nt. 24).
53. Ibid.
54. Ibid., pp. 258–259. Note from Bernard Susser, "The Behavioral Ideology: A Review and A Prospect," *Political Studies* (London: September 1974), p. 286.
55. Mitrany, *A Working Peace System,* p. 81, "The Way to Natural Selection."
56. Mitrany, *F.T.P.,* p. 258. Quoted from Mitrany, Mental Health and World Unity Proceedings of the *First World Congress on Mental Health,* Vol. IV, (London: 1948), p. 82.
57. Mitrany, *P.I.G.,* p. 172.
58. Ibid., p. 176.

CHAPTER TWO

The Evaluation of Functionalism by American Political Science

I
HANS MORGENTHAU

Professor Hans Morgenthau summed up the essence of functionalism in his introduction to the 1966 edition of Mitrany's *A Working Peace System*.

> According to Professor Mitrany, an international community must grow from the satisfaction of common needs shared by members of different nations. International agencies, serving peoples all over the world regardless of national boundaries, could create by the very fact of their existence and performance a community of interests, valuations, and actions. Ultimately, if such international agencies were numerous enough and served the most important wants of most peoples of the earth the loyalties to these institutions and to the international community would supersede the loyalties to the separate national societies and their institutions.[1]

To rephrase Morgenthau, functionalism is the effort to overcome political division, (for Morgenthau the division of the world into nation-states) by transferring people's loyalties to more useful international institutions. Professor Morgenthau judged this effort to be so important that "the future of the civilized world is intimately tied to the future of the functional approach to international organization."[2]

What are the problems of civilization and why is functionalism tied to its survival? In the course of a five page introduction,

Morgenthau presents a broad sociological account of the history of the modern world, diagnoses its fundamental ills and indicates why functionalism is the project of the future. According to Morgenthau, because the prime function of political power is the protection of the lives of the members in, and the way of life of, a human community, the feudal order was forced by its inability to withstand gunpowder and the first industrial revolution to yield first to the dynastic and then the national state. Sociologically, the same lack of protection which led to the collapse of the feudal order now confronts the contemporary world. Morgenthau contends that "the modern technologies of transportation, communications, and warfare, and the resultant feasibility of all-out atomic war, have completely destroyed this function of the nation state."[3]

At present, according to Morgenthau, three forms of nationalism oppose a rational response to the loss of essential functions by the nation-state. In the first place, traditional European nationalism has reasserted itself. Secondly, a type of nationalism understood as micronationalism has emerged in the new nations of the postwar world. This micro-nationalism is a reaction to the "congenital instability" of these new regimes. Finally, a third form of nationalism has emerged in the 20th century, which Morgenthau calls nationalistic universalism. Nationalistic universalism emerges out of a quasi-religious identification of the ends of one political regime with the ends of mankind. Though each of these forms of nationalism is explainable, they are not, individually or collectively, rational. The fundamental question of the current age, then, is how to move from our current situation, which is irrational yet pervasive, to a condition more suitable to modern technological and sociological conditions. Morgenthau contends that, "The only rational reply to the challenge which nationalism presents to the peace and order of the world is the voluntary cooperation of a number of nations with common interests for the purpose of creating supranational institutions after the model of the specialized agencies of the United Nations and of the European Communities."[4] Morgenthau judges that nations should cooperate in the creation of new, surpanational institutions. Nationalism in the modern age is irrational, supranationalism is rational. Morgenthau suggests an argument of reason by which to judge the political world. The judgment is that the continued existence of modern civilization is a rational end. A human desire to maintain the species, our individual lives, and a certain way of life dictates the response which Morgenthau advocates. Reasoning about our empirical condition dictates the response which Morgenthau advocates. Reasoning about our empirical condition dictates the value of functionalism.

To see the relation between Morgenthau's power politics and his support for functionalism, it is necessary to draw from a broader discussion of the problem than he provides in his introduction to Mitrany's work. *Scientific Man Versus Power Politics*[5] gives a clear expression of the relation between the two even though he does not discuss functionalism in the book. *Scientific Man Versus Power Politics* is Morgenthau's most philosophic exposition of politics. Most, if not at all, of what Morgenthau said about politics after 1946 has its basis in his earlier work. To compare what Morgenthau said about functionalism in 1966 with his elaboration of politics in 1946 ignores much of Morgenthau's other works. Since the exploration of why Morgenthau accepts functionalism as a rational alternative for man does not strictly coincide with his evaluation of functionalism's prospects, a more complete interpretation of Morgenthau's evaluation of functionalism will require reference to some of these works.

In *Scientific Man Versus Power Politics,* Morgenthau asserts that the "belief in science is the one intellectual trait which sets our age apart from preceding periods of history."[6] Assuming that man will successfully extend the method of the natural sciences to the social sciences, the typical political thinking of the age believes " . . . that if not now, at least ultimately, politics can be replaced by science."[7] Unfortunately, however, the rationalism which believes that science can replace politics misunderstands the nature of man, the social world and reason itself. It forgets that man is biological and spiritual, and assumes him to be simply rational.[8] In making this mistake about man, it distorts ethics and politics and perverts science.[9]

Rationalism is a generalized philosophy which fails to answer the questions of men who are placed in a world much different from the 18th century world in which rationalism has its roots. The temporary success of fascism indicates that people will and do reject the rationalism and liberalism of the intellectual elite, but the defeat of fascism in battle has given civilization another chance to provide answers to the questions of the people.[10] This opportunity suggests a re-examination of politics which takes its bearings

from the pre-rationalist western tradition. In particular, it "starts
with the assumption that power politics, rooted in the lust for
power which is common to all men, is . . . inseparable from social
life itself. In order to eliminate from the political sphere not power
politics—which is beyond the ability of any political philosophy or
system—but the destructiveness of power politics, rational facul-
ties are needed which are different from, and superior to, the
reason of the scientific age."[11]

We need not for our purposes here review all the failings which
Morgenthau finds with the applications of scientific politics. More
to the point is Morgenthau's discussion of the proper approach to
reasonable politics. In the context of a criticism of liberalism
Morgenthau begins to point to his view of reasonable politics.
According to Morgenthau, "Decadent liberalism still was convinced that democracy is peace and that autocracy, now resurgent
as fascism, is at least potential war. But whereas classical liberalism
had understood this opposition in the sense of different predominant tendencies of a nonexclusive character, decadent liberalism
gave this opposition a nonpolitical and absolute meaning. Hence
fascism and militarism, on the one hand, and democracy and love
for peace, on the other, became synonymous; and democracy
could not wage war without betraying its very principles to fascism."[12]
In such a circumstance the wars that liberalism fought in the 20th
century were necessarily ideological wars; prudent, but for impru-
dent reasons. The prudent man would admit that World War II was
fought not for "China, Ethiopia, Britain, or any other foreign
country, nor collective security, universal democracy, permanent
and just peace, but the influence upon the national interests,
expressed in terms of power politics, of violent changes in the
territorial status of these countries."[13] World War II was not fought
in order to secure rational ideals, but to secure power interests.
U.S. participation in World War II can be justified on the basis of a
reasonable calculation of interest, but the rationalist values by
which it actually justified its participation in the war are deficient.

According to Morgenthau the reliance of liberal politics on
rationalism and its faith in science were mistaken, even in suppos-
ing that science uncovered a calculable universe. "Matter has been
dissolved into electronic atoms; the traditional concepts of time,
space, and the law of gravitation have succumbed to the theory of
relativity; the quantum theory has transformed causation into

statistical probability and replaced determinism by the principle of indeterminacy."[14] If there is no determinism—as opposed to probability—in nature it is much less likely, according to Morgenthau, that it can be found in man. Social science can "indicate certain trends and state the possible conditions under which one of those trends is most likely to materialize in the future."[15] It, or its practitioners, cannot "predict social events with a high degree of certainty."[16]

The problem of the uncertainty principle for physics has an even deeper impact on social science: "In as much as nature is subjected to human action, it is the human mind which actually creates it, and the creation must bear witness to the quality of the creator."[17] "The human mind fulfills the same creative function for the social world."[18] Thus, "The social scientist . . . intervenes actively as both product and creator of social conditions."[19] In contrast to the rationalist interpretation, "The common element of which mind, nature and society partake is no longer reason pure and simple but reason surrounded, interspersed and underlaid with unreason, an island precariously placed in the midst of an obscure and stormy sea."[20] In any historical moment there are a limited number of political possibilities. "Ultimately the whole future of the social world appears to the analytical mind as a highly complicated combination of numerous systems of multiple choices which in turn are strictly limited in number. The element of irrationality, insecurity, and chance lies in the necessity of choice among several possibilities multiplied by the great number of systems of multiple choice. The element of rationality, order and regularity lies in the limited number of possible choices within each system of multiple choice."[21] Thus some sense of rational social planning is possible, but it is different from scientific planning.

In this milieu, "Reason, far from following its own inherent impulses, is driven toward its goals by the irrational forces the ends of which it serves."[22] Reason is not self-moving but is carried by interest and emotion "to where these forces want it to move."[23] The nature of reason is that it is a means to irrationally chosen ends. Nevertheless, "The conformity with, and hence the realization of, reason may become the main concern of interest and emotion."[24] Unfortunately, men who are driven in this direction cannot act in the world and when they attempt to do so end up in Hamlet's tragic circumstance.

Rather than attempting to make the human world scientifically rational the functions of reason in the social world are rather those of harmonization. "It (Reason) tends toward creating harmony among several conflicting irrational impulses. It brings ends and means into harmony with irrational impulses. It establishes harmony among several conflicting ends. It brings means into harmony with ends."[25] In the individual, reason will attempt to determine and to support the choice, within the context of each function, "most favorable to the survival, the growth, and the socially approved interest of the individual."[26] Nevertheless there may be, because not socially approved, reasonable choices which are never contemplated. The use of reason in the social sciences is always determined by what the particular social community itself is willing to let be investigated. Thus social science always involves "a moral choice between two extreme alternatives; the sacrifice of truth to the pressure of society, or the risk of earthly goods for the sake of searching for, and telling, the whole truth."[27] Modern rationalism, according to Morgenthau, does not understand the moral nature of social science.

"Man" according to Morgenthau is a political animal by nature; he is a scientist by chance or choice; he is moralist because he is a man. "Man is born to seek power, yet his actual condition makes him a slave to the power of others."[28] The moral issue of power arises from the necessity "of justifying and limiting the power which man has over man."[29] Some modern rationalists assume that moral action is a weighing of advantages and disadvantages of actions aimed at the greatest amount of human satisfaction (in which success becomes the primary judge). Others, of a perfectionist inclination, assume that the reverse process is true and thus elevate traditional ethics into a logically coherent system of thought (Kant) which is unbridgeably separated from human reality (even though the perfectionist does not accept the condition as inevitable).[30] The remainder of secular Western thought simply attempts to separate politics from ethics altogether, which results in "three fundamental attitudes: one proclaiming the permanent exemption of political action from ethical limitation; the second subjecting political action permanent ly to particular ethical standards; and the third, while recognizing the second alternative as a temporary fact, looking forward to the acceptance, in a not too distant future, of a universal ethical standard of which the private one is thought to be the model."[31]

In political fact men continue to subject politics to a standard, but the standard is one drawn from private life, including the standard that the end justifies the means (derived from the theoretical separation of public and private morality). Yet the truth is the only difference that exists between private action and public action is a relative one "without absoluteness. All human action is potentially immoral and political action is only a quantitative extension of private action in its effects."[32] All action is potentially immoral first, because no one can calculate completely the results of action; secondly, because to satisfy one demand on good intentions other demands must be sacrificed; thirdly, because the duty to be unselfish requires a certain amount of selfishness so that one can subsequently act unselfishly; and finally, because the *animus dominandi*, with which all men are born, urges a man to "maintain the range of one's own person with regard to the other, to increase it, or to demonstrate it."[33] The lust for power is limitless and is "of the same kind as the mystic desire for union with the universe, the love of Don Juan, Faust's thirst for knowledge."[34] Yet the attempt to realize it in practice always ends "with the destruction of the individual attempting it."[35] "The ubiquity of the desire for power . . . constitutes the ubiquity of evil in human action,"[36] and "to the degree to which the essence and aim of politics is power over man, politics is evil; for it is to this degree that it degrades man to a means for other men."[37]

Political and private action differ only in the degree of violation of the ethical norm. Yet, since politics deals most intimately with the realm of power, political success requires that ethics be violated, and a state acting in international politics merely represents the quantitative extension of the power drive in its citizens. It is limited only by a feeble normative order and the mechanics of the balance of power created by other similarly motivated states. Man according to Morgenthau (accepting completely Kant's formulation), is morally obligated to treat others not as "means to the actor's ends but as ends in themselves."[38] Thus everywhere and always man is evil, politics is evil, and international politics is evil. Since even inaction can be an action however, and man is therefore forced to act, he must choose the lesser of evils in any particular situation. Man is in a permanently tragic condition or antinomy which cannot be resolved. Evil is not an absence of something good but a permanent state. The prerationalists understood, as the rationalists do not, the "existence of two forces—God and the devil, life and death, light and darkness, good and evil, reason and passion—which struggle for dominance of the world."[39] Rationalism assumes that only more facts are necessary and solutions to social problems will be found.[40]

The truth, according to Morgenthau, is that, "Social problems such as marriage, education, equality, freedom, authority, peace, are of a different type. . . . They are the result of those conflicts in which the selfishness and the lust for power, which are common to men, involve all men."[41]

These problems are never permanently solved, they are only temporarily resolved. The temporary resolution of any particular problem—including that of peace—"depends essentially upon three factors:

> social pressure which is able to contain the selfish tendencies of human nature within socially tolerable bounds; conditions of life creating a social equilibrium which tends to minimize the psychological causes of social conflict, such as insecurity, fear and aggressiveness; and, finally, a moral climate which allows man to expect at least an approximation to justice here and now and thus offers a substitute for strife as a means to achieve justice."[42]

It is the task of the greater-than-mere-scientist statesman to create these conditions within the limits of the tragic situation of man (and therefore of the statesman). "Where the insecurity of human existence challenges the wisdom of man, there is the meeting-point of facts and freedom, of necessity and chance. Here, then, is the battlefield where man takes up the challenge and joins battle with the forces of nature, his fellow-men's lust for power, and the corruption of his own soul."[43]

We have gone into considerable depth in our recollection of *Scientific Man Versus Power Politics* in order to determine the analytic ground of Morgenthau's judgment concerning functionalism. In particular we have done so in order to see why Morgenthau suggests that functionalism is man's only rational alternative.

It is clear that Morgenthau does not expect science and liberalism automatically to solve man's problems. Liberalism and rationalism misunderstand nature, science, social science, man, and morality.

Considering as well that Morgenthau lumps Dewey and the pragmatists into modern liberalism, it would seem that Mitrany, a self-described pragmatist, would fall into the same group.[44] Nevertheless, there is a sense in which Morgenthau's realism is consonant with Mitrany's functionalism. Reason performs four functions for man. It harmonizes first, conflicting irrational impulses; secondly, ends and means with the irrational impulses; thirdly, several conflicting ends; and finally, means and ends. Though social conditioning may inhibit its activities, the reason of the social individual performs its functions with the survival, growth and socially approved interest of that individual as the objective. When a person acts, he sins (for one of his impulses to action is the ubiquitous *animus dominandi*), yet as a moral being man is still required to choose the lesser of evils.

Nationalism, according to Morgenthau, is an irrational impulse, a quantitative extension of the individual's *animus dominandi*. For the individual, nationalism may be not only a quantitative extension of his will to power, but, by transference, an end as well. Yet at two levels, the level of statesmanship, and the level of the individual, nationalism is an impulse or an end which reason can harmonize with other impulses or ends with survival, growth and socially approved interest in view.

Morgenthau tells us that the protection function of the nation-state has been destroyed by modern technology. He contends that "No nation-state is capable of protecting its citizens and their way of life against an all out atomic attack."[45] He amplifies this contention elsewhere saying that at the state level the use of conventional forces is still a rational activity, but, "The destructiveness of nuclear weapons is so enormous that it overwhelms all possible objectives of a rational foreign policy."[46] Furthermore, nuclear powers are limited in their use of conventional forces by the destructiveness of their arsenals, for escalation is always possible. Finally he contends that

> Instead of trying in vain to assimilate nuclear power to the purposes and instrumentalities of the nation-state, we ought to have tried to adapt these purposes and instrumentalities to the potentialities of nuclear power. We have refrained from doing so in earnest because to do so successfully requires a radical transformation—psycho-

logically painful and politically risky—of traditional moral
values, modes of thought and habits of action.[47]

Nuclear war and the danger of escalation in conventional war,
according to Morgenthau, threaten the survival of mankind. Thus
the transformation which Morgenthau discusses presumably stems
from his evaluation of the direction reason takes with respect to
survival. Nationalism is a legitimate or real impulse or end, but it
now runs counter to survival where nuclear weapons are concerned.
Furthermore, one might say that nationalism runs counter to the
individual's legitimate socially approved interest in material comfort (since transportation and communication operate globally). In
short, the destructiveness of war and the extension of technology
mean that nationalism at the level of the statesman has become
irrational. The nation-state which gathers up the *animus dominandi*
of individuals is therefore also irrational. The nation-state does not
protect life, therefore it cannot promote growth, and it reacts
contrary to the socially approved interests of individuals. As
Morgenthau says in *Politics Among Nations,* "One man may sacrifice himself for a principle but it is foolish and even morally wrong
for a state to do so."[48]

Why then is functionalism the rational alternative? According
to Morgenthau the problem of peace can never be permanently
solved. It's resolution at any one time depends on social pressures
which contain the selfish tendencies of human nature, a social
equilibrium which minimizes the psychological causes of conflict
and a moral climate which allows man to expect an approximation
to justice. Morgenthau, not entirely in agreement with Mitrany,
sees a transference of state functions to supranational institutions
(Morgenthau apparently qualifies functionalism out of a concern
for the *animus dominandi* in man and particularly its play at the
level of statesmanship). Yet the analysis offered by functionalism is
basically in harmony with Morgenthau's. Functionalism relies on
the social pressures of democracy, peace, and well-being to restrain
man, it works to create a social equilibrium—including a type of
social balance of power between functional institutions—which
minimizes the causes of conflict; and, if it meets its own expectations in any sense, it allows men to expect an approximation of
justice. Functionalism seemingly changes the institutional arrangement and therefore the direction in which the individual turns

in order to maximize his *animum dominandi;* it does not eliminate it.

The qualification which we introduced in the above paragraph deserves further consideration, however, for it indicates that Morgenthau is not as optimistic as is Mitrany about the prospects for functionalism, and further indicates an additional component to the equation for establishing a global society. Morgenthau argues in *Politics Among Nations* that, in addition to the sociological foundations of a political community, "Society has no substitute for the power of the Leviathan whose very presence, towering above contending groups, keeps their conflicts within peaceful bounds."[49] Thus, "There can be no permanent international peace without a state coextensive with the confines of the political world."[50]

A world state can only maintain itself if it gives humanity a legal personality, creates and keeps in motion agencies for worldwide social change, and establishes "enforcement agencies that would meet any threat to the peace with overwhelming strength."[51] According to Morgenthau, none of these conditions currently exists, though the first and the second come closer to having a sociological support than does the third. A world state cannot come into existence through conquest, federation, or education, according to Morgenthau, but the social basis for it can perhaps be laid by functional activity.[52]

In line with our qualification, Morgenthau equates functionalism with the gradual emergence of supranational institutions designed to perform specific functions which create a community of interests. Functions performed by the specialized agencies of the United Nations (the clearest current representative of functional activity) are too obscure to be noticed by most citizens. NATO, the European Community, and the agencies of technical and economic assistance have a higher profile, but NATO and the E.C. are regional. Furthermore, the extent to which NATO can create more than a sophisticated alliance still remains in doubt and the E.C., with its political purpose being to contain Germany, has not yet proven itself. Finally, primary economic and technical assistance agencies are so numerous, the projects to which they lend assistance so diffuse, and the perceived and actual motives and procedures of the givers so makeshift that little transfer of national loyalties can be expected.[53]

Morgenthau concludes that

> We proposed that the first step toward the peaceful
> settlement of international conflicts that might lead to
> war was the creation of an international community as
> foundation for a world state. We find that the creation of
> an international community presupposes at least a mitiga-
> tion and minimization of international conflicts so that
> the interests uniting members of different nations may
> outweigh the interests separating them.[54]

The means by which those conflicts can be minimized are, according to Morgenthau, the traditional diplomatic activities of states.

The bearing of this discussion on our qualification is of some
importance. If the only way that functionalism can work is to
eliminate conflict by laying the foundations for a world state, and
if the functional agencies must become supranational as stepping
stones to that world state, and finally, if even the prospect of
creating functional agencies depends on prior, broadranged political accommodation, Morgenthau and Mitrany may not share the
harmony of positions that we have suggested. We are not sure that
Morgenthau's qualification is decisive with respect to his consideration of functionalism, but it is a point necessary to consider.

In any case, it does not seem that Morgenthau anticipates a
world without tragedy in the functional future. Tragedy is a function of the individual's will to power interacting with the moral law
to treat each as an end, not as a means. Therefore, functionalism
does not do away with the dilemma of the individual or of the
statesmen (or for that matter, with the need for political prudence).
Functionalism permits survival. Therefore, it also permits the dialectic of morality and power to continue. On the basis of Morgenthau's critique of liberal reason, his re-articulation of what he
considers to be the correct pre-rationalist understanding of reason,
his analysis of man and the relation between man and reason, and
his analysis of the historical situation of contemporary man, he
concludes that the impulse of nationalism and the nation-state
which contains and extends it are irrational from the standpoint of
survival, growth, and interest. Among the few available options
open for choice in any given historical circumstance, reason's
harmonizing function tells us to choose survival over nationalism,
and perhaps functional organization over the state. Functionalism
may see the proper place of man in the world. Man is both a

creation and a creator. Therefore functionalism offers a reasonable alternative for man. The alternative may or may not be
progressive but it does permit human life to continue. The social
scientist fulfills his moral purpose by making this choice clear. The
individual and statesman make it a free choice.

II
INIS L. CLAUDE JR.

Claude explicitly examines functionalism as an "Approach to Peace."
Thus Claude's discussion of functionalism is motivated by a similar
but not the same intention as Mitrany. Claude notes this when he
identifies functionalism "with such values as prosperity, welfare,
social justice, and the 'good life', rather than the prevention of war
and elimination of national insecurity,"[55] but he goes on to point
out that in many cases these ends are not determinative of the rank
of ends, but tend to be justified in terms of making men peaceful.

Claude identifies David Mitrany as the chief exponent of
functionalism. As Claude says, "The theory of functionalism, which
is essentially an assertion and defense of the proposition that the
development of international economic and social cooperation is a
major prerequisite for the ultimate solution of political conflicts
and elimination of war, has been most elaborately developed and
persuasively stated by David Mitrany."[56] As we have noted, Claude
discusses functionalism from the standpoint of a slightly different
question than Mitrany asks. Claude's question is, what does functionalism have to say about organizing a peaceful world? Mitrany's
question is, what are the needs of the contemporary world and
how may they best be met? Now in the sense that a peaceful world
might be the most important need of the contemporary world the
two questions converge. But they are not the same. A peaceful
world might not be functional. In the short term, functionalism
may not solve the problem of war. Be that as it may, Claude
examines Mitrany's idea of functionalism as a possible means of
achieving peace, and he is not far different in perspective from the
Mitrany who says that war is now irrational and the world cannot
be made peaceful, or be held together, by force.

The method of functionalism, says Claude, may be summa-

rized by delineating separability theses and doctrines. The first
Claude calls the separability-priority thesis. "It involves the assumption than human affairs can be sliced into layers, that the concerns
of man are so stratified that economic and social problems can, in
a preliminary fashion, be separated from political problems and
from each other. Having adopted this assumption, functionalism
then proceeds on the theory that the treatment of economic and
social matters should take priority."[57]

Secondly, Claude identifies "the doctrine of transferability,
expansibility, ramification, spillover or accumulation." Though
Claude significantly does not cite Mitrany here he does point out
that "Some have argued that most men, having learned the arts of
fruitful international cooperation at the level of technical or economic problems, will transfer their new skills and habits of mind to
the development of collaborative solutions at the highest political
levels."[58] Whether this is, in strict terms, taken from Mitrany is
questionable though Mitrany does seem to suggest that from time
to time.

According to Claude, functional theory regards war "as the
product of the objective conditions of human society."[59] "In the
second place, functionalism attributes the phenomenon of war to
the institutional inadequacy of the nation-state system."[60] Beyond
this, functional theory purports to provide an indispensable labora-
tory for the experimental development of organizational patterns
and techniques which may serve as models for the ultimately
necessary machinery of internationalism at the highest political
levels."[61] Finally, "Functionalism envisages its tasks in terms of the
alternation of the subjective conditions of mankind." That is,
functionalism, "by focusing attention upon areas of common interest,
builds habits of cooperation which will equip human beings for the
conduct of a system of international relations in which the expectation of constructive collaboration will replace that of sterile conflict as the dominant motif."[62] Functionalism relies for its success
both on man's rationality and man's irrationality. It finds a new
enemy for man in "poverty, pestilence or ignorance." Furthermore
it expects that men will "forget" their political difficulties once the
habit of cooperation has developed. Nevertheless, functionalism is
rigorously rationalistic in its expectation of a "transfer of loyalties
to the international community in response to the growing usefulness of functional agencies."[63]

Claude says that functionalism is attractive because it appeals not only to pacifists but also to "humanitarian idealism and to rational self-interest." "It asks governments not to give up the sovereignty which belongs to their peoples but to acquire benefits for their peoples which were hitherto unavailable, not to reduce their power to defend their citizens but to expand their competence to serve them."[64]

Functionalism also appeals to conservatives by its organicism and evolutionary nature, and to the liberal because it is distinctively modern and progressive. "Mitrany writes like a social democrat, and he finds his great inspiration in the New Deal's notable invention, the TVA. Functionalism represents the application of the welfare state philosophy to the international sphere."[65] Finally, "functionalism has all the earmarks of a profound and sophisticated approach to the problems of war."[66] It is not superficial and offers no panaceas.

The essential element of Claude's critique of functionalism as a theory is skepticism. Claude is skeptical about the asserted economic causes of war, and about the proposition that economic organization can replace political organization as the primary mode of human living together. In the first place, one would need to know precisely what phenomena are political and what are economic—a distinction which is not readily observable. Even if such a distinction could be made, however, Claude doubts the possibility of transfer of loyalties (which are not always grounded in a calculation whose primary objective is the satisfaction of a rationally determined economic interest). Thus, with respect to Mitrany's contention that the time has come to separate our spiritual life from our material life, Claude legitimately questions, without flatly denying, the possibility of doing so.[67]

In a second vein, Claude is skeptical about the feasibility and advisability of stratifying or compartmentalizing economic activity. Mitrany's functional concept takes account of the danger involved with this activity and counters that the function itself limits the effects of such stratification. That is to say, particular functional arrangements will rise and fall with the need for the function itself. Once a function is superfluous, the organization of activity addressing that function will fade with the function itself. On the basis of political experience at the national level, Claude casts doubt on this functional conclusion. Experience suggests that organizations are far from limited by their original purposes. Furthermore, experience suggests that the fluidity of social and economic processes is endangered by the stratification inherent in organizing a function. That is, the process is endangered by the creation of too many parts which may or may not work harmoniously.[68]

Haas had contended that Claude rejects the separation between power and welfare leaving the rest of functionalism unexamined and implicitly leaving himself nowhere to turn for theory except back to Realism.[69] At least from a theoretical standpoint we can see that this is not quite the case. Claude brings to light reasonable questions which a man of good will can legitimately ask of functionalism. Experience to date is not always comforting to the functionalist, and if we are to see his propositions as an approach to peace we would not wish to do so with one eye closed. Claude never tells us that a functional world is impossible though he does think that it is unlikely.

Yet, as we have noted, Claude's interest in functionalism is as an approach to peace, not as the source of propositions whose operationalization will permit us to predict integration and will make the study of international relations scientific. In short, the real point Haas made is that he and Claude do not agree about the nature of theory in the study of international relations. Claude seems to be much closer to Mitrany's view of theory than does Haas. Though Claude offers no solution to the problem of peace which might be compared with Mitrany's functional concept, his critique of functionalism, as well as other approaches to peace, is not that of a disinterested spectator. Claude's objectivity emerges not by divorcing himself from the world which he views but precisely by placing himself within that world by way of a concern for peace. (A concern, we might add, which is not indifferent to whether peace is established or not).

Claude does not simply reject the possibility of a functional world, nor does he embrace the theory. Rather he leaves the possibility as one whose actuality will be determined by history. Since functional propositions suggest the possibility of a transformation in human behavior our experience of man in the nation-state cannot give us decisive answers to the questions which we ask of the theory. Claude does, however, begin the task of evaluating functionalism as it had proceeded in practice.

As a practical experience Claude gives functionalism mixed reviews, though the reviews do tend toward the negative. Claude notes that the diversity and independence of the functional system made efficiency very difficult. A part of this problem is, according to Claude, that of "sovereignty consciousness" and "empire building" on the part of the various independent functional agencies. Further Claude notes the tendency of the Economic and Social Council of the United Nations to create its own "institutional offspring."[70] Claude points out that "If conflict is the major problem of international political organization, confusion is an equally serious problem in the functional sphere."[71]

Yet Claude also notes that, out of the confusion, units like the Administrative Committee on Coordination have "made important contributions to the effective meshing of the parts of the complex system,"[72] and goes on to suggest that "in the final analysis, the profusion of international agencies may be evidence of the vitality of the idea of international community, and the confusion may simply prove that multinational institutions, like national ones, are owned and operated by human beings. . . . "[73]

Claude secondly points out that "functional agencies have experienced difficulty in concentrating on important matters," or put differently, "maintaining a reasonably clear and restricted focus on international activities."[74] Yet here he also notes that "as in the case of the coordination problem, the steadily growing emphasis upon programs designed to promote economic development has contributed to the mitigation of this tendency."[75]

As indicated above, Claude is critical of the presumed separability of the political and nonpolitical (power and welfare). The clearest lesson of United Nations experience is, according to Claude, that "functionalism's assumption of the preliminary separability of political and nonpolitical matters does not hold true—not in this generation, at any rate."[76] In particular, Claude points to "two great political struggles," the cold war and the colonial question, which dominate the generation and, "have both impinged sharply upon functional operations."[77] At the time Claude wrote, U.S. dominance of the United Nations decreed that functional programs would be anti-communist in the first instance, and, "secondarily a device for alleviating the tensions of the struggle over colonialism."[78] Since the Soviet Union was basically uninvolved in functional activities at that point, the agencies became "excessively reliant upon the support, and particularly the financial support, of the United States."[79] In this way the agencies were, in effect, harnessed to U.S. policy. But Claude notes another interesting, and perhaps in the long run more important, point involved in U.S. dominance.

The power of the U.S. in functional organizations "exposed them (the organizations) to the internal political peculiarities of the American scene."[80] Congressional control of American purse strings kept agencies under close supervision and led to efforts to "extend Congressional patronage privileges to international organs."[81] Secondly, "The political issues of states' rights and untrammeled free enterprise are also transmitted by American predominance to the international functional system. . . . "[82] "International coopera- tion," Claude goes on to explain, "in economic and social fields requires the participation of national governments which have sufficient domestic authority in those fields to be able to cooperate. This is precisely the status that jealous champions of states' rights and defenders of pre-New Deal free enterprise wish to deny to the federal government of the United States."[83] Claude suggests that, "Given the various bases of hostility toward functional enterprise which exists in the United States, including the reaction against the political mentality which was epitomized by the New Deal, it is perhaps surprising that the United States should be a participant."[84] To the extent that U.S. participation in functional organization is not paradoxical, however, Claude also contends that the U.S. attempts to extend its control to activities in areas where it does not need a fuller extent of control. That is, it finds it impossible to stay out of other people's business. This is a point which Mitrany discusses in the context of the breakdown in the theoretical separa- tion between the public and private realms in the modern world.

Despite these immediate difficulties, however, Claude does not deny that possibility or the desirability of the long term project. He concludes that "The actual achievements thus far are substantial and significant, even though not spectacular, world-shaking or world saving. Above all, the record to date indicates that func- tional activity is at least in the short run more dependent upon the political weather than determinative of the political weather."[85]

I would like to isolate a few aspects of Claude's critique of functionalism. In the first place, Claude's examination of function- alism in practice tends to confirm his critique of functional theory. The politics of the cold war and decolonization have deeply affected the progress of functionalism. Furthermore the coordination of the sectoral agencies has proven to be a problem. Yet Mitrany is talking in terms of a new conceptualization of the political universe equivalent to that which arose during the Renaissance and the Reformation.

Mitrany suggests in *The Progress of International Government* that men of goodwill, in particular political scientists of goodwill, should get on the bandwagon of functionalism. Morgenthau tends to agree. That is, Mitrany says the greatest function which the political scientist can now perform is not an analytical function but a normative function. According to Mitrany, however, there really is no difference between the two functions. If we assume that Claude is a man of goodwill we are led to wonder why he does not jump on the bandwagon and even goes so far as to counsel skepticism. To add to our difficulty we may also note that Mitrany seems to assume that at least one of the sources of change in the world is a change in opinion. He says that nearly everyone jumped on the Grotian bandwagon and that this change of opinion helped to create the state system. If ideas play a leading role in political affairs, should not the political scientist be an advocate, not simply an analyst? Should he not turn his attention to showing not only where reality makes the fulfillment of an idea difficult but also to showing political men how they can surmount the difficulty?

Yet it might equally be asserted that the soundness of the functional idea has not been demonstrated. At best functionalism is a well-intentioned opinion. Analysis shows some grave difficulties with the theory in its confrontation with the real world. In fact, there are enough difficulties to persuade us that only a wait-and-see approach is possible. We will wait and see how functionalism fares in its competition with other ideas, and in its confrontation with the political world. By willingly discussing the idea we will keep it alive in the minds of men but advocacy would assign a value to functionalism which has not been demonstrated. In fact, the fate of functionalism really lies with active political men. If they are persuaded either by its theory or its practice functionalism will have proven itself. If not, advocacy on our part could not help it any way.

There seems to be a basic difference between Mitrany and Claude concerning the educative role of political science. Mitrany says that the purpose of political science is to make clear the relation of things. Yet this purpose includes an aspect of consciously creating those relations. On the other side, we see an educative function performed, not by shaping the mind to a new idea, but by shaping the mind to the existence of political conditions, which impinge upon the fate of ideas, both positively and negatively. Claude performs a function which Mitrany, because he sees the solution as an integral part of the analysis, cannot perform. Nevertheless Mitrany seeks to perform a function which Claude's skepticism cannot perform. For those who, in their goodwill, accept the rationality of Mitrany's argument, Mitrany shows the way forward beyond the contradictions of the age. This function cannot be performed except through a teaching, if you will, a prophecy.[86]

III
JAMES P. SEWELL

We now turn to our third commentator on functionalism, J. P. Sewell, whose book, *Functionalism and World Politics,* was clearly sympathetic to functionalism as formulated by Mitrany. After reviewing the functionalist thesis Sewell subjects the argument to criticism. He notes a series of minor questions one could pose about the approach. How can one really define a problem? How does one know when it is solved? He notes that "a problem (any problem) implies both a situation observed and the observer who designates that situation a 'problem.'"[87] How, Sewell asks, does one reach an actionable consensus on a problem or know when it has been solved? The difficulty, says Sewell, is solved by letting the material element of "technical self-determination" enter through the back door of "felt common need." Technicians may be able to define a problem but their definition and solution may not solve the human problem which brought men together. People may be able to agree about a need but the technical solution may not solve the human problem.[88]

  This points to a second problem in functionalist analysis—that of the breakdown in representation. On a mechanical level we can say that the transmission belt of felt needs as they are conveyed to the unit which satisfies them (government) has, on the state level, broken down. Mitrany says that the new functional way can provide better transmission and better solutions than the old state system. Mitrany proposed a representative functional assembly composed of experts which could serve as a transmitting system. Sewell questions whether, in this solution of Mitrany's, there is sufficient guardianship of the guardians. Is there "sufficient provision even for need—or problem—reportage?" Are common problems synonymously equatable with the world of deeds and motives? Furthermore, there is little that is similar in Mitrany's scheme to the notions of competitive representations and constitutional checks and balances as they have emerged in the West, and in particular, in the U.S.[89]

These two difficulties add up to a deeper problem for functionalism. Its concern with techniques over people fails to account for politics as the life of a people. Functionalism does not show how or why new norms will be generated or come to be among the population. Functionalism makes a mistake in regarding the economic or social categories as substantive[90] and leaving politics as a residue. Though he notes that Mitrany is willing to use politics for his non-political ends, Sewell suggests that Mitrany would stamp as much of the political as possible out of life.

This finally points to an "inadequate appreciation of obligation." Functionalism "falls short of providing an adequate basis for interpreting the origin and status of present international institutions."[91] If one understands politics as "the rationalization of the exercise of power by and upon society," he must first decide what is meant by rationalization. One could understand it in the Weberian sense of economy or efficiency.[92] "When the functionalists address the objective aspect of problem solving, when they employ such terms as 'technical self-determination'—and this is most of the time—they seem to have in mind essentially this style of power rationalization."[93]

In a second sense, however, rationalization can be understood as justification—in particular "the justification of power's use on human beings; specifically the justification of its employment by society upon itself." This means legitimization or obligation ("insofar as those upon whom power impinges are in a position of choice in determining the legitimacy of its exercise.")[94] In practice, according to Sewell, one segment of society imposes itself upon the rest of society while the justification of this practice ranges from defending the state's essence in its monopoly of violence to defending the law as custom. In between these extremes the opportunity for most political philosophy emerges when one can ask not only what is, but what should be. Politics is the "range of publicly relevant activities between what one is obliged by necessity to do or not do, on the one hand, and what he feels obligated to do or not do, on the other."[95] The functionalist rejects obedience by force but does not count simply on custom as the source of legitimacy of obedience. "Mitrany's expectation is far from that associated with traditional society, with its solitary constitution and ascriptive ties. The functionalist model is *Geselleschaft,* not *Gemeinschaft . . . ,*"[96] and "Man's choice is assured by multiple access to the associations of the modern world."[97] The only means of, or reasons for, obligation that functionalism offers are

1. Man's obligation to certain types of norms stems from the technical ability which was exercised in their formulation.
2. Man should follow because of the benefits which accrue thereby to him and his fellow beings.[98]

Sewell concludes that we may tentatively express disappointment at the functionalist conception of obligation; for nothing in it really obligates man to anything except himself. In short, to Sewell it is a *Geselleschaft,* not a *Gemeinschaft.*

Sewell expresses this disappointment more pointedly in his concluding chapter. "My own critique can be reduced to two themes. The first is commitment. It is a manifestation of that activist impulse which the functionalist argument appears to encourage and yet, paradoxically, tends to subvert."[99] That is, it attempts to have people commit themselves emotionally to a goal whose object is purely rational self-interest. "The second theme is purpose— that which provides for commitment to a longer and higher view, and thus informs its striving with a sense of direction."[100] Sewell points to Robert Redfield's dichotomy between "technical order and moral order," (the moral order is more than the technical order which results from mutual usefulness, as from the mere utilization of the same means). By this standard Mitrany is too pluralist and too liberal. That is, he is too willing to settle for a purely "technical order." The "functionalist argument had purchased non-controversiality at too dear a price."[101] As Sewell asks, within the context of a functional-technical order,

What can fulfill the integrative role of the space-bound and territorially oriented "citizenship' while at the same time taking account of newer relationships between modern man, his several territorial domains and his involved social universe to which the functionalists draw our attention?[102]

Sewell, in short, is sympathetic to the functional idea but judges that it ends in over-emphasizing the material over the human, the technical over the moral.

Let us examine this argument briefly. Claude noted that functionalism depends both on rationalism and irrationalism in man, though in a certain sense it fundamentally demands of man a rigorous rationalism with respect to his self-interest. Sewell not only acknowledges this point but is quite critical of it for it elevates the technical over the human. Yet, from a humanist perspective one cannot take this criticism as decisive, at least not in its stated form. The technical is at least as human as those activities which Sewell describes as the human. As the result of man's calculation, rationality, and inventiveness, the technical is in some senses the precise distinction between man and the rest of the animals. While morality and conscience are equally considered to be human, the variations in morality which we see distinguished in the world lead us to question whether they are as fully representative of humanity as is his potentially universal technical order. Since there is no universally recognized moral order we are led to wonder whether morality is not sociological, while the technical order, resting on the reason which distinguishes man from the animals, is not the truly human order. Thus a humanist might argue.

Mitrany has an "out" which does not require us to adopt a critical attitude towards Sewell's understanding of the human. All that is required for Mitrany is that man conform to his self-interest and permit technicians to address it. "Space-bound territorially oriented citizenship" will find a counterpart in the higher workings of the spiritual-cultural life of communities no longer distorted by the state. Presumably the only spiritual activity no longer permitted will be that of Plato's "spirited" warrior class. At least this activity would be severely circumscribed into some police function. Whether Mitrany provides an outlet for human natures of this type or whether they, along with the state, will wither away is perhaps a deeper question, yet one that Mitrany does not answer precisely.

The reception of Mitrany by political science thus ranges from Morgenthau's claim that rationality demands functionalism, to Claude's view that rationality requires scepticism toward functionalism, to Sewell's contention that at least technical rationality endangers truly human, though not necessarily rational, living. In Chapter 3 we will discuss Mitrany's reception by political science from a slightly different angle. Ernst Haas examined functionalism but was really interested, not in the critique of the theory, but in its transformation. The nature of Haas' intended transformation was ambiguous however. In one sense he hoped to transform the character of international relations by changing the way we think of it. To do so Haas attempted to subject the study of international relations to scientific operationalization, which assumes manipulation based on knowledge. But, Haas claimed that he did not care what, if anything, was done with the knowledge he articulated. Mitrany's functionalism may legitimately question whether Haas' "transformation" provided any new substance for the theory. Furthermore Mitrany's functionalism was not indifferent to the possible uses of knowledge (if Haas, in fact, demonstrated significantly new theoretical insights).

NOTES

1. Hans J. Morgenthau, Introduction to *A Working Peace System,* by David Mitrany, p. 11.
2. Ibid.
3. Ibid., p. 9.
4. Ibid., p. 10 emphasis added.
5. Morgenthau, *Scientific Man Versus Power Politics.*
6. Ibid., p. 4.
7. Ibid.
8. Ibid., p. 5.
9. Ibid.
10. Ibid., pp. 8 and 9.
11. Ibid., pp. 9–10.
12. Ibid., p. 70.
13. Ibid., p. 74.
14. Ibid., p. 132.
15. Ibid., p. 136.
16. Ibid., p. 137.

17. Ibid., p. 142.
18. Ibid.
19. Ibid., p. 143.
20. Ibid., p. 145.
21. Ibid., p. 151.
22. Ibid., p. 154.
23. Ibid., p. 155.
24. Ibid., p. 156.
25. Ibid., p. 158.
26. Ibid.
27. Ibid., p. 165.
28. Ibid., p. 168.
29. Ibid., pp. 168–169.
30. Ibid., p. 172.
31. Ibid., pp. 175–176.
32. Ibid., p. 188.
33. Ibid., p. 192.
34. Ibid., p. 194.
35. Ibid.
36. Ibid.
37. Ibid., p. 195.
38. Ibid., p. 196.
39. Ibid., pp. 201–203.
40. Ibid., p. 205.
41. Ibid., pp. 205–214.
42. Ibid., p. 215.
43. Ibid., p. 217.
44. Ibid., p. 223.
45. Ibid., pp. 4, 14, 28, 30.
46. Mitrany, *A Working Peace System,* p. 9. This is of course not a judgment unique to Morgenthau, as Claude has expressed the same sentiment, "The conclusion is inescapable, that a high priority on the human agenda must be assigned to the task of achieving maximum safeguards against both the penultimate tragedy of the smashing of human civilization and the ultimate tragedy of human extinction." Power and International Relations, p. 4. Claude also points out, however, that if peace is purchased at any price, survival "may be both empty and precarious, for masters of slaves can revoke the right to live as well as the rights that make life worth living." p. 5. Yet, "values without survival are no more meaningful than survival without values." p. 5. For an interesting comparison see Joseph Cropsey, "The Moral Basis of International Action," Robert A. Goldwin, ed., *America Armed,* (Chicago: Rand McNally Co., 1963), pp. 71–91.

47. Morgenthau, *Scientific Man Versus Power Politics.*
48. Morgenthau, *A New Foreign Policy for the United States,* p. 208.
49. Morgenthau, *Politics Among Nations,* p. 493.
50. Ibid., p. 499.
51. Ibid., p. 502.
52. Ibid., pp. 504–513.
53. Ibid., pp. 513–525.
54. Ibid., p. 525.
55. Claude, *Swords Into Plowshares,* p. 378.
56. Ibid., p. 379.
57. Ibid., p. 384.
58. Ibid.
59. Ibid., p. 381.
60. Ibid., p. 382.
61. Ibid.
62. Ibid.
63. Ibid., p. 385.
64. Ibid., p. 386.
65. Ibid., p. 387.
66. Ibid.
67. Ibid., pp. 387–388.
68. Ibid., p. 388.
69. Haas, *Beyond the Nation-State,* p. 24.
70. Claude, *Swords Into Plowshares,* p. 396.
71. Ibid., p. 397.
72. Ibid.
73. Ibid.
74. Ibid., p. 398.
75. Ibid.
76. Ibid., p. 399.
77. Ibid.
78. Ibid., p. 400.
79. Ibid.
80. Ibid., p. 401.
81. Ibid.
82. Ibid.
83. Ibid.
84. Ibid.
85. Ibid., p. 407.
86. We cannot take this question further at this point. Nevertheless it
can be recognized that the prophet and the philosopher represent
a problem not only in a religious age but apparently in a non-religious
age.

87. Sewell, *Functionalism and World Politics,* p. 37.
88. Ibid., p. 39.
89. Ibid., pp. 41–42.
90. Ibid., p. 43.
91. Ibid., p. 45.
92. Ibid.
93. Ibid., p. 47.
94. Ibid.
95. Ibid., p. 48.
96. Ibid., p. 49.
97. Ibid.
98. Ibid., p. 50.
99. Ibid., p. 330.
100. Ibid.
101. Ibid., p. 329.
102. Ibid., p. 332.

CHAPTER THREE

The Reformation of Functionalism

Among the political scientists known as the neo-functionalists, Ernst Haas has come closest to identifying his research with Mitrany's functionalism. This identification came by way of his analysis of and critique of functionalism in *Beyond the Nation-State,* which is related to, but not the same as, his work on integration. It has often been contended that Haas leveled decisive criticisms at parts of Mitrany's functionalism while retaining and clarifying that which was truly valuable in the approach.

We maintained in the first chapter that functionalism retained its value as an approach to understanding international organization, but did not deal with the contention that *Beyond the Nation-State* had superseded functionalism with a more precise and a more sophisticated analysis.[1] We are not convinced that *Beyond the Nation-State* really improved on Mitrany. We do think that *Beyond the Nation-State* was a useful and well-intentioned examination of functionalism in theory and practice. But some of Haas' arguments seem to make functionalism say something that it does not say and to ignore the importance of some of the questions which are vital to functionalism. This is natural, for each interpreter of a political theorist reacts somewhat differently to the text used as the basis for interpretation. Haas, more than our first three interpreters, not only interpreted functionalism but changed it. The change emphasized functionalism as the tool of integration, not as an approach to solving human problems.

The interpretation which Haas brought to functionalism consisted of three parts. First, Haas attempted to show the ideological and normative aspects of functionalism. Secondly, Haas attempted to rewrite functionalism into scientific language and, in the process, eliminate the normative and ideological parts of functional theory. By rewriting functionalism he intended to give functionalism a new role to play in the study of international relations, which went beyond the stale prescriptions and analysis of realism.

We will examine Haas' reformation of functionalism by asking three questions. First, we ask, what does Haas mean by ideological functionalism? Secondly, how does Haas reform functionalism? Finally, we inquire whether Haas successfully turned functionalism to his new purpose?

The spirit of Haas' criticism of Mitrany may usefully be summarized before proceeding. Haas says that Mitrany is not sufficiently scientific. From this general criticism more specific criticisms follow. Because Mitrany is insufficiently scientific he has created a doctrine, which, though interesting, contains several serious errors of analysis. Accordingly, Mitrany's work and his project are suspect. Haas' project is to correct the major flaw of Mitrany's work by joining it to, or grafting it onto, a contextual analysis of social phenomena which is scientific within the capacity of the subject matter to submit to science. The contextual analysis to which Haas joins functionalism is already a hybrid, however. It " . . . combines historical sociology with a political type of structural-functional analysis which can make use of empirical studies of political situations and the already available insights of organizational theory."[2] This multi-hybrid will, according to Haas, tame Mitrany's flights of fancy and permit his basic propositions to be studied in a methodical and predictive manner. This new approach may not "bring international order out of the chaos of national confrontation," but it "can tell us in which direction the faint ripples of common concern are likely to spread,"[3] — a task which the old functionalism could not perform.

The main obstacle to offering such a hybrid approach, according to Haas, lies in the conceptual difference between Mitrany's functionalism and structural-functional analysis as it was developed by anthropologists and sociologists. Mitrany sees his system "as a concrete set of relationships in which actors participate consciously; to Merton as to Nadel, a functional system refers to 'observable objective consequences' of action from the standpoint of the observer. Juxtaposing these two viewpoints involves a merger of concrete and analytical systems."[4] The difference between the two is, of course, important to Haas. Mitrany's approach involves the analyst in subjective judgment whereas the Merton/Nadel approach permits one to step outside the system and, therefore, to analyze the system objectively. Mitrany's approach, despite its clear distaste for ideology, leaves itself open to the dictates of personal whim and world views because it has no means of denying the observed a concrete relationship to the observer, and vice versa. Functionalism is not objective science, but is tainted with opinion.

I
THE IDEOLOGY OF FUNCTIONALISM

Haas says that the ideological and rhetorical nature of functionalism can be examined if we group the thought of functionalists into four "issue areas." These areas are "their view of the Human Condition, their criticism of the nation-state in relation to individual fulfillment and international conflict, their theory of change, and their program of reform."[5] Let us look at what Haas says about functionalism in each issue area.

With respect to functionalism's view of human nature, Haas contends that functionalism is ideologically grounded in Guild Socialism and Pluralism. Functionalism is further described as naively believing that man is "good, rational and devoted to the commonweal."[6] Anyone who writes to offer rational argument or analysis of human things assumes that people are capable of hearing and responding to the analysis or argument. But that is not really what Haas seems to be saying about Mitrany here. Rather, he thinks that functionalism is naive about human nature in a more specific sense. Functionalism may understand that most people are guided by self-interest and will, far more often than not, put the good of self over the good of the whole. Thus, self-interest is the source of government, which makes authoritative decisions to adjust conflicting self-interests, and it gives politicians a purpose, for they compromise and accommodate the many self-interests in society to each other.[7] But, the administrators and experts themselves have interests, and to expect them to be able to overcome politics because of their dedication to expertise and the self-satisfaction of a job well-done is Mitrany's specific naivete.

Functionalists secondly argue, says Haas, that the fact that politics interferes with the common good "brings into focus the distorting role of the modern state with respect to the possibilities of human fulfillment."[8] According to functionalists, states do not serve human fulfillment because they "unnaturally" interrupted the "pre-industrial and pre-national occupational groups" which "were the true focuses of human happiness because they afforded a sense of participation in the solution of practical problems."[9] To the functionalists, work, not power, is the fundamental component of a fulfilled and creative life. With respect to the politics of international relations then, " . . . the peace of statesmen, of collective security, of disarmament negotiations, of conferences of parliamentarians, of sweeping constitutional attempts at federation, all this is uncreative. It is so much power instead of creative work."[10]

Haas thirdly discusses the functional theory of change. He describes the "how" of the change to the new order as "in the starkest and most abstract terms . . . a purely systemic one."[11] By taking advantage of "converging technical interests" a new system will be made in which these "interests will become fused."[12] The functionalist thesis contends that fusion will occur by way of "an automatic process of change once the initial carving out of converging task contexts has taken place."[13] Haas sees in the functionalist view a dialectic in which the " . . . thesis of national exclusiveness can be outflanked by the antithesis of creative work dedicated to welfare, yielding the eventual synthesis of world community."[14] The only human choice which is available in the process is the fact that man can undergo a learning process. Since the technical skills which will lead the way into the new era will still be responsible to the General Will of the community, "the answer to maximizing the learning process lies in extending the range of participation in practical problem solving."[15]

Haas concludes his summary of Mitrany's functional ideology in terms of functionalism's "program of reform." His authority here is Engle who says that "These three features—a reliance predominantly upon functional units, an expectation of an eventual system of government made up primarily of interlocking functional units, and the assumption that in functional cooperation certain dynamic behavioral mechanisms of an 'institution-building' and 'consensus-building' nature are at work—constitute the ideal type of the functionalist theory at the international level."[16]

Haas tells us that the weakness of ideological functionalism is evident in practice. Functionalism's ideological propositions failed in two historical case studies: The World Health Organization and Arms Control. Functionalism as an ideology cannot explain the growth of the WHO because that growth does not originate in a decision to take health out of the political arena. Nor does a test of functionalism show that the role of the expert is crucial, for international arms control, as often as not, involves experts who speak primarily from the standpoint of their nation's advantage.[17] However one might take Haas' description of ideological functionalism; Haas assumes that the description and criticism of ideological functionalism is really just a step on the way to the real discussion. The real discussion, which isolates the most important contentions of functionalism, takes place at the level of theory not ideology.

II
THE REFORMATION OF FUNCTIONAL THEORY

A. Functional Theory

There are two important aspects of Haas' analysis of functional theory. First, Haas says that functionalism "separates notions held to be as one by Realists and thus hopes to arrive at a totally different conception of the world from the now dominant Realist conception." Secondly, Haas asserts that integration rather than conflict will be the "central pillar" of the new functionalist world.

1. Separability

The separations which Haas identifies take the four following forms: the separation of power from welfare; the separation of various governmental tasks into discrete elements, even if temporarily, but military-defense is completely separated from economic-abundance tasks; the separation between the political and the technical which leads to the conquest of the political by the economic and the suspicion of the activities of the government as opposed to voluntary groups; and finally, the separation between the loyalties imprinted on the political actor. Mitrany asserts that loyalties are created by functions and can change. In doing so he seems to deny any existing hierarchical supremacy of nationalism, even though in other contexts he seems to deplore this supremacy.[18]

Haas ascribes to functionalism a Marxist perspective with regard to the origin of war. That is, war arises from economic scarcity. If we solve the problem of scarcity, the problem of war will be solved. The integration of the new world is made possible by the utilitarian self-interest of men who cooperate when interest dictates it. Competition is not necessary; it arises from national scarcity. Thus men need to learn that their interests are best served when they cooperate to overcome scarcity.

Although there are several minor problems which Haas has with functionalist theory (such as its imprecise definition of community, its imprecise articulation of the members of the community, its inadequate discussion of precisely what functions will need to be performed in a functional world, and its attempt to disguise a mechanical system in emotional language) he contends that the real difficulty for functionalism in its Mitranian form is that it cannot contend with Realism's critique of the separability doctrines. It is because Mitrany has inadequately formulated the separability doctrines (in addition to the fact that Mitrany is normative and ideological) that functionalism needs to be reformed.

The realists easily assert "the primacy of the political and take for granted the presumed hard outer shell of the sovereign nation-state."[19] That this criticism is nearly telling is evident in the criticisms of functionalism by Engle, Sewell, and Claude (who are not realists), who "reject the theoretical assumptions of functionalism in no uncertain terms by denying the adequacy of the separability propositions to sum up the potentialities of human development."[20] Their critique is essentially that power and welfare are not separable in that "commitment to welfare activities arises only within the confines of purely political decisions."[21] One functional decision does not necessarily lead to the next. Furthermore, technical decisions are so only in light of a political decision; hence, voluntary groups are not likely to have a great effect in international relations. "Most important, Claude and Engle deny that loyalties develop from the satisfaction of needs, and can be separated and rearranged so as to ignore the nation."[22] Finally, Sewell's analysis of functionalism goes considerably beyond these points in attacking the 'liberal' and 'pluralist' dreams implicit in functionalist thought."[23]

According to Haas, criticisms like these give up the ghost to realism without being necessarily "realist" themselves. In fact, within the original realist criticism, instances can be shown where functionalism and realism approach one another. Functionalism, in criticizing power admits power, while some realists, such as Kenneth W. Thompson, modify the victory of power and admit ethics, or at least explanations of actions posited in ethical language, as the tribute vice pays to virtue.

But, as a theory of politics, realism is moribund, and if approached correctly, the separability doctrine may show how functionalism can be used as a tool to "get [international relations thought] beyond the blind alley of Realist analysis."[24] A refined functionalism is the perfect way to bring international relations into the mainstream of social science.

2. The Integration Linkage

By fusing functionalism with historical sociology Haas says, "it is precisely our hope that functional sociology can show how *Gesellschaft* can develop into *Gemeinschaft* (taken in Tonnies' sense)." For Mitrany " . . . community is immanent in the evolutionary logic of his action process and hence a notion of integration is implicitly part of his theory."[25] The refined separability doctrines will coincide with the integrational thought of historical sociology. Integration in historical sociology consists of:

> Mutually supporting inputs into a social system [which] tend to be associated with growth of structure, expansion of functions, development equilibrium.[26]

Haas' use of the concept "refers exclusively to a process that links a given concrete international system with a dimly discernible future concrete system."[27] Thus, "integration would describe a process of increasing interaction and mingling which obscures the boundaries between the system of international organizations and the environment provided by their nation-state members."[28] Functionalism fits into this notion of integration because it avoids "the analytic rigor of assuming the existence of some systemic equilibrium;" because it avoids the "trap of assuming complete freedom of the will" (since each epoch sets the environmental conditions of the next); and because in its formulation functionalism is at least compatible with the view of historical sociology "in which systems are always concrete and always defined by the concerns of the epoch's actors."[29] Yet, for Haas the functions exist for the sake of integration, and are not crucial in their own right. The purpose of the adaptation thus changes, not only the language, but also the meaning, or intention, of functionalism.

Historical sociology is a form of analysis in which motives, not structure, can be typified, and "the context is the typical interplay of typical aspirations—the wholeness of the situation analyzed is provided by its predominant hopes, fears and styles of conduct."[30] Thus, successful integration can be detected in a transformation in motives. Haas' project seeks to combine Mitrany's propositions concerning a future system with a form of historical analysis. The hybrid, functional sociology, will permit the projection of functionally defined motives into the future because it has been disciplined by a methodology. In the wake of this effort, the propositions which Mitrany's approach offered to the student of international relations correspondingly go through their own modification or revision. How are these propositions to be revised?

> First, we must revise the theory of interest that the Functionalist uses, a theory that apparently misreads through the eyes of nineteenth-century Liberals the intent of the founders of modern Western Liberalism. Next, we must strip the utopian elements from the group theory of the Functionalists and amend their separation of expert and politician, state and society, so as to reflect the integrative potential of actual modern practices, this in turn requires the insertion into functionalist thought of a more highly structured theory of law than is now present. We hope to emerge with a revised series of separability doctrines that portray international organizations as a species of institutionalized interest politics, capable, on the basis of empirical systems theory, of transforming the international system.[31]

B. The Reformation

Before we analyze this revision in detail a comment is necessary. The above paragraph illustrates a confusion which is an inherent part of Haas' analysis, specifically, his lack of clarity as to whether international organizations are "a species of institutionalized interest politics" which *will* transform the system, or whether in order to do so they must be understood—by both analysts and actors—on the basis of structural-functional sociology before they can do their work effectively. That is, even though he eschews prescription his theoretical activity is constantly looking to prescribe.

Let us return then to the revision of functional theory. Functionalism, according to Haas, misunderstands the nature of interest. Thus he returns to earlier criticism of the functional understanding of interest as either "hopelessly utopian or rigorously mechanical." According to Haas, the problem of interest is vital to the functionalist project because only an adequate theory of interest can hope to explain why experts are going to introduce us to the "blessed state of world community." The utopian character of the theory of interest articulated by functionalists is the result of its pluralist origins and its dependence on the " . . . Durkheimian notion that only voluntary groups can 'drag' isolated individuals into the 'general torrent of social life,' " and, " . . . overcome the anomie of modern man and result in creative work toward the common good."[32] But work toward the common good presupposes a common good or common interest both nationally and internationally. Functionalists tend to see this common good in a universal concern with welfare and, further, insist "on the therapeutic magic of participation. . . . " But, the problem of getting from here to there raises, according to Haas, difficulties with which functionalists are not really ready to deal, for Haas says flatly that there is no demonstrable recognition of the common good as welfare.[33]

Furthermore, a simple mechanical translation "of the values of advancement of welfare and the protection of democratic rights . . . would under current circumstances demand a set of priorities subordinating these to the need for military security." Only a prior solution to the security question can permit action on the welfare and rights questions. The functionalists cannot show how a world concerned with security will turn into one concerned with welfare and rights because they have no articulate theory of interests to ground the mechanical passage from one set of interests to the new set.[34]

Since there is not a mechanical solution to international community-building, the functionalists, according to Haas, are forced to rely on the role of manipulative experts in moving the world from A to B. Haas rejects the notion of a simple and natural harmony of interests because there are obviously conflicts of interests between groups. Nor are these conflicts entirely overcome by positing a key role for manipulative experts. By positing the leadership of experts, argues Haas, Mitrany must also subject the experts, or leaders of voluntary groups and governments, to the interests of their particular organizations and the organizational personality and mystique that each organization fosters. Thus, any inability of the experts to agree endangers the project for the same reason that the groups themselves may endanger Mitrany's project. There are no real mechanisms for restraining either the particularism of the group or the particularism of the experts who represent the group. In Mitrany's argument everyone must agree about both the problem to be dealt with and the way in which that problem is solved.[35]

Though this problem is insoluble in Mitrany's terms, Haas says there is a way it can be overcome. The way lies in the articulation of a theory of interest which takes account of the lessons provided by the founders of liberalism. The founders of liberalism (Locke, Smith, etc.) had abstracted " . . . the pursuit of economic interest from any imputed concern with the general welfare, systemic equilibrium or social order, thus permitting the natural and opposing interaction of interests in an impersonal market to determine the shape and evolution of the social system."[36] The founders of liberalism, unlike the Marxists and unlike Mitrany, did not assume an automatic progress, nor did they determine a way to show objective interest. "What men *felt* to be their interests was good enough to make the system work."[37] In morals the economic answer sufficed as well. What men *felt* to be their moral interests was good enough to make the system work. For the liberals both economics and morals " . . . originated in instinct, desire and passion; and neither was the result of action intended to advance the good of society as a whole." A notion of interest based on this lesson would serve the functionalist thesis better than Mitrany's current utopian/mechanistic impasse. According to Haas, "A functionalist theory of converging but separate purposes, partaking of some general notion of welfare would ring truer than a utopian vision of technocratic progress based on identical interests."[38]

Haas makes a further addition to his corrective of Mitrany, for he is not entirely satisfied with the narrow concentration of the older liberalism. The older liberalism had still permitted a great deal of social control of non-economic interests. For Haas, an interest is basically anything that any group or individual claims is an interest. As Haas summarizes his argument,

> We further reject the notion of conscience, good will, dedication to the common good or subservience to a socially manipulated consensus on welfare questions as possessing little consistent reality in living politics. Cooperation among groups is thus the result of convergence of separate perceptions of interest and not a spontaneous surrender to the myth of the common good. Furthermore interest goes well beyond the liberal separation of *economic* interest from the restraining force of *society*. Any claim made upon the community on behalf of the values dear to some group represents an interest even though substantively it may refer to religious education, residential zoning, reforestation or the prevention of cruelty to animals.[39]

Taking this view, or theory, of interest has the further virtue of recognizing that because interests do not change significantly over time, the groups are constrained by a certain determinism inherent in the world, prohibiting groups and leaders from hypothetically changing their interests overnight. Interests can change, but the logic of the real world suggests that they do so only slowly.

If one is willing to accept Haas' revised theory of interest, the mechanical and educational variants of functionalism may have something to say, for out of the possible overlap of interests between groups, " . . . certain kinds of organizational tasks most intimately related to group and national aspirations can be expected to result in integration *even though* the actors responsible for this development may not deliberately work toward such an end."[40] The revised interest theory can thus " . . . point the way toward the identification of group aims and the resulting interaction that may give rise to integration based on the unwilled, or imperfectly willed, separate demands and claims that enter the arena."[41] Functionalism sensitizes us toward spotting the "pattern" of interaction as it arises. Functionalism needs a semi-mechanical theory of interest in order to explain how the potentially converging interests which it spots for us can actually give rise to integration.

Haas, secondly, says that the functional analysis of groups needs to be refined. Haas rejects Mitrany's preference for voluntary groups as opposed to state action. Groups do not constitute the whole of meaningful social action. They are, according to Haas, simply one of the "carriers of the integration process."[42] Mitrany's emphasis on voluntary or associational groups leaves the functionalists out in the cold in a world which is not predominantly composed of pluralist-industrial-democratic nations. What is needed in a world ranging from totalitarian to competitive multiparty systems is a specification of the "types of groups which can be expected to enter the process."[43] This is a task which Haas finds best reserved to functional/sociological analysis based on the prediction of possible converging interests. That is, the functional theory can be refined by also positing as significant groups both government *and* "associational" groups. Furthermore, the activity in which cooperation occurs needs not be considered primary to all those affected. Since a specific group is not the sum of social life for an individual in the way a guild organization would be, the organized interest in which the group participates can link the participants together and integrate their concerns without committing the group members to a new primary, or even secondary, loyalty. This is the crucial point from Haas' perspective, for through it we finally get beyond Realism. The refinement of interest theory and group theory permits one to see that the separability doctrines are not absolute but relative to the interests of groups and actors at any particular time and place.

Haas, thirdly, notes a need for a refined theory of law if functionalism is to be at all helpful to his predictive science. Mitrany assumes the compatibility of the various conceptions of welfare "while neglecting the role of law in providing a normative procedure for settling differences."[44] Unless the common good is systemic, equilibrium and understanding of an accidental common good is necessary. Modern nations form ascriptive ties on the basis of symbols, meaning that a *Gemeinshaft,* or community, is composed of people who agree on the means for attaining welfare, if not the substance of welfare, and that is the form of their community. An international community is absent because there is no agreement on means. In short, and related to Haas' rejection of the common good, Mitrany does not show a means of making authoritative decisions in conflicts between group values.[45]

To Haas, functional legal theory would appear in this manner: the "task of this type of legal theory then is not merely the explanation of how, why and owing to whose action norms are accepted in a general sociological context; it also involves an explanation of how, why, and owing to whose purposive or unintended actions the norm expands and eventually integrates the disparate social systems into a more closely knit whole."[46] He continues:

> Based on assumptions reminiscent of the Functionalists, this type of law is seen as flowing almost automatically from social and economic interaction, which is brought about by organizational necessity and "imminent need." The law is therefore non-formal, non-legislative, and devoid of any general or abstract rules. While it need not dovetail with the power aspirations of state, neither is it contradictory to them. It co-exists with them. International conflict prevents the emergence of norms based on general consent; therefore this type of law "just grows" because the antagonists experience a need for it despite or because of their antagonism. Society is pictured everywhere as no longer directed toward individualism and the defense of individual autonomy, but toward the fostering of coordinate man organized with others for the achievement of specific ends.[47]

C. Revised Functional Theory as Functional-Sociology

To Haas, Mitrany's functionalism had been valuable, not because it was sound analytically. Rather, it contained certain vague propositions of interest, which could be reformulated into something of use to the student of international relations. Once reformulated, functionalism might offer the political scientist the opportunity to analyze, systematically, international relations and organization, and to predict with some accuracy the course of international integration. The type of system or method of analysis that is "capable of linking functionalism to integration theories (and thereby giving it discipline) is a *concrete, actor-oriented* abstraction on recurring relationships that can explain its own transformation into a new set of relationships, i.e., into a new system."[48] Mitrany's system had dotted no *i*'s and crossed no *t*'s; it had merely asserted the necessity of such a transformation.

Haas' adaptation of functionalism permits one to identify the true items to which functions are imputed—policy demands—based on the perceptions of the actors themselves. By an examination of words and actions the observer can rigorously determine the "true" motives and purposes of the actors, and in the process define functions as those actions "noted by the observer that tend towards integration of the system."[49] Thus one can measure both the extent to which integration is taken as a purpose and the extent to which the activities undertaken tend toward integration. This further permits the things done or said out of a sense of purpose to be distinguished from the actual integrating function performed, if it is performed. Mitrany's functionalism failed to distinguish between purpose and function, creating an inherent ambiguity in the notion of function. Integrating functions or activities might be undertaken with no thought to integration. Alternately, an integrating purpose or intention might not give rise to integrating activities or functions. Functional sociology, by separating the two when it looks at concrete actors and actions, permits a more disciplined and empirical description of what is really happening. Functional sociology also permits one, once the true items or functions are determined, to determine the units which are served by the functions—in this case the units served by the functions are governments and groups. Finally, functional sociology permits one to show the mechanisms through which purposes and functions must be fulfilled—organizations, contacts, etc.[50]

III
HAAS AND MITRANY ON FUNCTIONALISM

In the light of the influence of the attempt to bring scientific rigor to functionalism some evaluation of that attempt is necessary. The initial difficulty we face derives from Haas' treatment of the normative aspects of functionalism. The examination of ideological functionalism rejects functionalism as a norm, or a teaching, yet demands from it an explanation of how we will move from A to B. Mitrany's work (see Chapter One and Chapter Two on Claude) has an explanation of how we will move from A to B, and it has a demonstration of this explanation based on our experience as a civilization.

Mitrany is a progressive and pragmatist. As such he assumes that human nature is the product of experience. Presumably we may know human experience and also see from what activities an improvement in human living might derive. Thus the project of his pragmatism is basically the continuing creation of man based on learning from experience. In this sense Mitrany could be said to have examined the sources of our experience (2500 years of Western civilization) and developed not only a theory of change but a recommendation as to the course that change should take.[51]

We may see a similar difficulty with respect to Mitrany's understanding of the common good (though it is not evident that the competition between the individual and the community to define the good has ended). We suggest that Mitrany never really misunderstands human nature, and thus the common good, in the way Haas says he does. Far from ignoring self-interest and interest group politics Mitrany identifies interest as one essential ground of the functional project. Haas never advances beyond the concept of interest in his understanding of politics. For Haas, the adjustment of interest is the essence of politics. In this sense, then, Haas and Mitrany are in analytic and normative agreement. The distinction Haas would have had to make in order to offer a genuine criticism of Mitrany is between the ends of self-interest (narrowly understood) and the ends of the ambitious who desire not just to exercise power but to exercise it for the sake of glory or ideology. These are the people Mitrany castigates, for, in ignoring their interests, they have become unreasonable. His ideology of human nature is, in that sense, no more ideological than Haas' scientific understanding. In a sense, Mitrany goes beyond Haas' understanding of human nature for he at least acknowledges the existence of different motivations, and further understands that men respond to those motivations, in different ways in different times and places.

More to the point, Mitrany's understanding of "human nature" is historical. Haas should have discussed and examined this understanding in an evaluation of the functionalist theory of change. Mitrany has in mind a change in perspective equivalent to that associated with the Rennaissance. He contends that there is an essential difference between feudal politics and liberal politics, and that we, again, are in an equivalent era of change out of liberalism. Mitrany certainly seems aware of the fact that the administration of public functions is necessarily political. In that sense politics and self-interest will necessarily continue. Yet he maintains that the kind of politics that created the nation-state is inappropriate to an epoch when the nation-state has lost its essential purpose, just as barons and knights and feudal loyalty are inappropriate to a world which is, in principle, republican and democratic.

We may see a third aspect of our difficulty in evaluating Haas in his suggestion that, for Mitrany, the state is an interruption of the earlier and future way of human being. While Mitrany certainly grants a special status to work, functionalism is not a call to throw off the state and return to the old ways. It is a call for new ways. The state currently interferes both with creative work and with creative living because it no longer responds to its founding purpose, not because it is an aberration. That is, to Mitrany, the state's actuality implies that in an earlier epoch it did correspond to a basic human purpose. Furthermore, while the work group will certainly be an important association in the functional world, perhaps even the primary association, it can equally be said that, for functionalism, working together in the material world is the precondition of other more fruitful activities and group identifications. If we extend the concept work to include the purposeful things one does, that is, actions undertaken to place one's imprint on the environment (an activity which creates and perpetuates the individual in time), then the universal "need to earn a living" (or work) becomes but one case in a series of activities the functionalist deems to be warped by the nation-state. (It is then the whole range of active life and the associations which arise from that active life, which are now disturbed by the state). More precisely, the state is not an unhealthy interruption of an otherwise continuous determination of human being by work activities, but a humanizing activity or project from an earlier era which is now an anachronism but still the precondition of any future human activities.

Though Mitrany, by training, certainly was no stranger to dialectic reasoning, it is doubtful, and nowhere to be seen in his writing, that he considered functionalism to work in the purely abstract dialectical manner which Haas describes. We submit that he would not have counted on functionalism to "outflank" the state—more accurately, if functionalism is dialectical, it will develop within the state as the state's negation, resulting in a qualitatively different human organization (universal in scope with human loyalties related to universal functions rather than to the type of universality associated with "nation-states").

This criticism may be boiled down into a more general criticism. The problem with Haas' discussion of Mitrany's normative approach is that it nowhere takes account of the influence of political thought on history. This is, of course, a controversial topic and one to which Haas is not indifferent. He tells us in undertaking his criticism of ideological functionalism that he wants to eliminate its ideological aspects because ideological considerations, or false opinions, have been so destructive in human history. But when Haas examines Mitrany's functionalism he takes little account of the influence which Mitrany's thought might have on the future. To the extent that Haas does take the future effects of Mitrany's thought, as opposed to his description, into account it is in order to minimize it. Let us here only indicate the consequences for Haas of his decision to reject thought as a formative aspect of political reality.

Haas undertakes his critique of Mitrany in order to formulate the propositions necessary, if not sufficient, to an analysis of international integration which will be predictive. Functional propositions will show where integrative processes are likely to spring up. Now it is the case that, if the interests of states and individuals overlap today, in Haas' understanding there must also have been times in the past when they overlapped. In most cases these concerns probably have not led to integration, though one can use the American example as an instance when they did. Regardless of the shared interests of the American states, they would not have united, or at least we cannot know that they would have united, if opinion had not been led in that direction by a group who constituted at the same time both a political and an intellectual elite in the bodies politic. That is to say then that American integration depended on the preparation of public opinion, and without leaders dedicated to "integration" it was not a foregone conclusion. It is not clear that economic and social interests drive events in any particular direction without mediation or even direction by opinion makers.[52]

Once an opinion maker or political man who represents the opinion maker takes up an issue such as integration he is free to move as a Jean Monnet and as a Charles DeGaulle. The question then is more than locating the points where interests will converge in the future and involves the analysis of how an important idea or goal enters into and directs activity towards its attainment. Mitrany says in *The Progress of International Government* that after a metabolic change struck Western civilization in the Renaissance/Reformation, political theorists set about to articulate in thought the nation-state and that, whether or not they were contemporaneous, practice at least did not advance without collateral advances in thought. As we have indicated in our discussion of normative functionalism, Haas does not examine Mitrany's understanding of history which is where one sees Mitrany's theories of change, human nature and the common good. Is history mechanical? For Mitrany it is organic. Is there freedom of the will? Certainly people are free not to solve their social problems, but there is a certain irrationality in taking such a position. Are experts important? Of course, to the extent that they are men of good will who put their expertise to the service of the social and rational good.

This point links into the question of the proposed reforms suggested by functionalism. Haas' characterization of the functional reform is essentially accurate. Yet since he has eliminated the educative role of the political scientist and sees the reform as some sort of automatic process, Haas misunderstands the inner process of functionalism (though he adequately describes its formal process).

If Haas thus took issue with the ideological nature of functionalism on the basis of an insufficient account of that ideology, his criticism of theoretical functionalism suffers from much the same problem. The extent to which functionalism incorporates a Marxist

view of war is at least debatable. Indeed, it is not economics which
cause war in the functional view. Economic or social cleavage may
be the proximate cause of wars, but even these wars occur because
political structures have not adapted to changed social circumstances. Since peaceful change is possible and is practiced from
time to time even in international relations, the cause of war is
more easily understandable as a failure of political adaptability.
Such failures may take the form of rigid adherence to formal
structures, to ideology, or to national separatism. Of course, to say
this does not entirely remove Mitrany from the Marxist perspective (politics as the epiphenomenon of economic substructures),
yet, nowhere does Mitrany say that modern wars are necessary as a
result of the bourgeoisie's slavish devotion to capital. It is hardly a
peculiarly Marxist perspective to say that war has a close relationship to economic conditions.

At another level, we may say that Mitrany understands that
wars are not fought simply over economics understood as material
well-being. They are also fought over the objectives of power,
glory and ideology. This point certainly links up with Haas' identification of a utilitarian calculus, for Mitrany contends that if such
ends (motives, desires, pursuits) ever were useful for man, power
(power understood as an objective unrelated to its social utility),
glory, or at least military glory, and ideology are useful no longer.

But this is a normative assertion, not a theoretical or value free
proposition. That is, Mitrany indicates that wars have seldom been
useful for man, and today they certainly are not. Man has reached
a point in his evolution where he can abandon war as a human
activity. To the extent that scarcity begets conflict states stand in
the way of ending wars because, in principle, scarcity has been
overcome through technical advances, and states now limit the
application of these advances.

Mitrany's emphasis on interest is also important from the standpoint of the distinction between cooperation and competition.
Interests as opposed to ideologies can be reconciled or adjusted.
Interest politics seem to constitute Mitrany's understanding of
rational politics. Thus the problem of competition versus cooperation can be determined on the basis of utility, though Mitrany leans
toward the cooperation end of the spectrum. In this sense it
certainly is true that Mitrany moves beyond analysis to advocacy.
If interest politics are rational politics the process by which we

move beyond the nation-state depends on an educative process which orients people toward material well-being.

The nation-state has already accomplished this task internally (which is why Mitrany says that theory is silent with respect to municipal politics and that practical interest adjustment reigns supreme), therefore Haas' effort to reduce Mitrany's argument to a science of integration misjudges Mitrany's argument at a crucial point. More accurately than to say that integration is to be the central pillar of the new system, we might say that the extension of an implicitly universal concern for material well-being beyond the borders of the nation-state forms the central pillar of the new system. Integration may follow the concern, it does not guarantee it.

Finally, with respect to the separability doctrines, which Haas says are totally different from the realist understanding of the world, we must add some caveats before moving on. The first two doctrines are collapsible into the third. Power, the military defense function, politics, and government are accordingly distinct from welfare, economic-abundance tasks, the technical and economic and the work of voluntary groups. Perhaps Mitrany's earlier writings on these questions are unclear (Mitrany himself admits that there was a misunderstanding).[53] But, whatever the source of this misunderstanding, there really is a distortion involved in these separations. The key to unlocking this misunderstanding turns on the role of the public and the private, the distinction between which, Mitrany says, has collapsed. If there is not a principled argument over whether an activity should be performed publicly or privately, it is not a question of separability between power and welfare, defense and economic abundance, voluntary groups and government, political and technical-economic tasks, but a question of the most practical way the public can organize its necessary functions. For example, the economic does not conquer the political; rather the political or public uses the economic/technical in order to pursue its rational interest in welfare.

The fourth doctrine presents a slightly different problem. If analysis tells an individual that the state does not fulfill its intended function, it would only be rational for him to deplore it. Whether loyalties can be shifted from nation-states to agencies which fill material interests is questionable, but if the current situation is irrational there is no reason to continue intellectual support for that situation. Thus, it is not surprising that Mitrany should refuse to grant a rationally pre-eminent status to nationalism as opposed to his admitted recognition of its contemporary ubiquity. A condition such as the hierarchical supremacy of nationalism can exist regardless of whether it remains rationally justified. The international community of which Mitrany speaks is hardly that of the familiar village, but it does not deny the need for ascriptive ties—it substitutes the experience of nationality for the experience of nationalism (in other words it depoliticizes nationality). Such a spiritually oriented community would in practice be identifiable in the mutuality of its functions and satisfactions on behalf of the national groups.

In understanding the public as necessarily political (as dealing with the affairs of the community) Mitrany seeks to align organization with its concerned public, its functional tasks, but not to destroy or overcome public life. Any political thought which sees the political process as the adjustment of self-interest (which takes into account both the reality of common interests and the reality of competition), in contrast to accommodating pride, ideology, and the desire for political glory into its outlook, accepts Mitrany's basic assumption about the character of the new order. Whether such a politics is rigidly deterministic and mechanical or whether it is rationally free activity—taking into account the determinate limitations inherent in any particular environment—is a matter of interpretation. This point finally links us to Haas' contention that integration is the purpose of functionalism. Mitrany simply tells us that there is no purpose to political discourse and political science if there are no solutions to political problems, and that the ubiquity of the nation-state is currently our most severe political problem. The nation-state may be communitarian and democratic, that is, its citizens may accept the proposition that in some sense their welfare is also dependent on the welfare of the community, and the state arbitrarily limits the well-being of its members. In defining integration as the purpose of functionalism rather than rational well-being Haas overlooks the true pillar of the new order, which is the materialistic and democratic character of the epoch.

IV

HAAS AND MITRANY ON REFINED FUNCTIONALISM

In our above discussion we suggested that Mitrany's understanding of the meaning of interest politics is not much different from that of Haas but also that it is broader and more historical than Haas is willing to acknowledge. Haas merely says that economic and moral interests do not have to be consciously shared in order to make way for integration and that this integration can emerge through a context of competition as easily as through a context of cooperation. The argument that Mitrany misreads liberalism is wrong, not because Mitrany really agrees with earlier liberals such as Locke and Smith, but because he contends that their theory was incomplete and at the level of the nation-state has been overcome both theoretically and practically. The public functions and the private functions have been fused and will not be separated again in the immediate or indefinite future. The distinction between private interest and public interest does not hold up. To argue against Mitrany on this point requires more than counterassertions about liberal analysis because, to Mitrany, this analysis was as normative as is functional analysis. Behavior which developed under the umbrella of that thought will necessarily resemble it, and the truth of human personality means there is a partial truth enclosed in liberal thought, but it is not the entire truth of man's political behavior. In short, for Mitrany, the liberal analysis of interest is an ideology as much as is his.

Haas opposes the notion of the common good; "cooperation is the result of separate perceptions of interest" and that interest should be seen as "any claim made upon the community on behalf of the values dear to some group. . . . " Haas further objects to the functionalists' preference for private groups, their reliance on groups as the essential element in social action, and their lack of specificity as to what groups are likely to enter into the integration process— particularly given their preference for "associational" groups as opposed to purely public groups. In this combination of refined interest and refined group theory Haas attempts to show that cooperation emerges out of a rational calculation of interest which is not a common interest, but one in which different actors, be they groups or governments, participate for specific and various reasons. Thus any functional organization represents not a coalesced or common interest in a function, but an overlapping of interests which is simply reducible to the parts that overlap. Such an interest then has no boundaries of its own; it is rather an infinitely separable collection of interests. Success of an organization then has everything to do with the extent to which the organization as a body desiring growth can give itself the character of a legitimate interest and play its own role as an interest among many, public and private. In this view the necessity of the function itself is lost to the analysis of integration potential. What for Mitrany is seen as the universality of the objective function is subjectivized into the interests of various actors. Further, the realization of the purpose which gives rise to the function is no longer primary or even important. The serious question becomes whether the organization, once created, can, by asserting its own interest, expand its tasks, encompass more overlapping interests, and thereby integrate the actors in the sense of performing more actions together. From the functional perspective Haas' activity constitutes a conceptual dissipation of the purposes of functional organizations which makes rational choice impossible for political people. Other than the growth of organizations, there is no real purpose to Haas' functionalism, for it no longer makes any difference whether real needs are to be satisfied or not.

That a form of integration is not inimical to Mitrany's functionalism is clear from even a superficial reading of his work. That integration rests on the possibility of substantial purposes is implicit in Haas' interest in moving "beyond the nation-state." But there is no fusion of the two types of analysis. For Mitrany, the functions and purposes themselves, because they have coalesced into the self-sustaining concept of a particular need, are the substance of functionalism. Integration or universality is then seen as an interest or purpose, but restricted to, and by, the universality of conceptual need itself. Whether the function is carried out "associationally" or inter-governmentally is a practical question, but is not decisive with respect to the question of whether a function needs to be performed or not.

By casting functionalism into the mold of an ideology, Haas had cast doubt on the empirical or "scientific" validity of functionalism. In short, Haas raised an essentially epistemological argument against Mitrany. Mitrany never addressed Haas' argument specifically but he did leave hints and suggestions as to his position with respect to the status of that argument. In "Retrospect and Prospect," Mitrany says that the "quality of science is to give a more exact insight into how things work under certain conditions; it is founded upon constants which impose their own unity upon all working in a particular field."[54] Mitrany says further that the purpose of political science is to make clear "the relation of things."[55] One of the peculiar aspects of international relations is that it is too turbulent to be reduced to constants which can make the human future strictly predictable. He also claims, however, that even if functionalism was held to a purely scientific standard it would be judged more scientific than the plethora of new methodologies currently used to study international relations.[56] He finally asserts that " ... those who would find a way out by trying to make politics 'scientific' cannot have forgotten that from the classic Greeks to this day only those have penetrated its mysteries who always strove to think as humanists."[57]

Haas had seen a problem when he pointed out the difficulty of combining a concrete system with an abstract analytic system. His refinement of functionalism deprived the concept of a concrete relationship with the world.

NOTES

1. J. Boyan Callestio and Harold Burnham, "Eurocontrol: A Reappraisal of Functional Integration," *Journal of Common Market Studies,* Vol. XIII, No. 4, January 1975, p. 348.
2. Haas, *Beyond the Nation-State.*
3. Ibid., p. 497.
4. Ibid., p. 25.
5. Ibid., p. 8.
6. Ibid.
7. Ibid., pp. 30–35.
8. Ibid., p. 9.
9. Ibid.
10. Ibid., p. 12.
11. Ibid.
12. Ibid.
13. Ibid.
14. Ibid.
15. Ibid., p. 13.

16. Ibid., pp. 13–14.
17. Ibid., pp. 14–18.
18. Ibid., p. 21.
19. Ibid., p. 23.
20. Ibid.
21. Ibid.
22. Ibid.
23. Ibid.
24. Ibid., p. 24.
25. Ibid., p. 26.
26. Ibid.
27. Ibid., p. 29.
28. Ibid.
29. Ibid.
30. Ibid., pp. 29–30.
31. Ibid., p. 30.
32. Ibid.
33. Ibid.
34. Ibid., pp. 30–31.
35. Ibid., pp. 31–32.
36. Ibid., p. 33.
37. Ibid.
38. Ibid., p. 34.
39. Ibid.
40. Ibid., p. 35.
41. Ibid.
42. Ibid., p. 37.
43. Ibid., p. 38.
44. Ibid.
45. Ibid., pp. 39–40.
46. Ibid., p. 43.
47. Ibid.
48. Ibid., p. 77.
49. Ibid., p. 83.
50. Ibid., pp. 83–85.
51. Mitrany, *P.I.G.,* p. 139.
52. "With public sentiment, nothing can fail; without it nothing can succeed. Consequently he who moulds public sentiment, goes deeper than he who enacts statutes or pronounces decisions. He makes statutes and decisions possible or impossible to be executed." Abraham Lincoln, "First Joint Debate, Ottawa, August 21, 1858," in Robert W. Johannsen, ed. *The Lincoln-Douglas Debates* (New York: Oxford University Press, 1965). Whether this could be considered Mitrany's

reasoning is open to question yet his account of the influence of
Grotius, Machiavelli and other political theorists indicates a similar
view. See Mitrany, *P.I.G.,* p. 25: Machiavelli's The Prince "gave a new
turn to political theory."; p. 27: Bodin's "doctrine of Sovereignty gave
a working body of philosophical reason to this state,"; and p. 30: "the
doctrine of Grotius provided a philosophical meaning and purpose
for the budding international order."
53. Mitrany, *F.T.P.,* p. 261, and note 31.
54. Ibid., p. 247.
55. Ibid., p. 65, and note 24.
56. Ibid., pp. 247–248.
57. Ibid., p. 266.

CHAPTER FOUR

A Re-Evaluation of Functionalism

Our analysis of functionalism has taken us through the critiques of Morgenthau, Claude, Sewell, and Haas. Morgenthau seemed to be in essential agreement with Mitrany. Claude questioned Mitrany deeply about the possibility of building political accord on the basis of economic accord. He further questioned the ability of functionalism to create, organize and dismember parts in accordance with need and efficiency. Finally, he points out that neither state's rights nor economic individualism have been suppressed in the United States. This fact would seem to indicate that the public and private are not so fully intertwined as Mitrany indicates. Sewell questioned Mitrany's rationalism, wondering whether a functional world could be a human world. Haas basically criticized functionalism for its failure to demonstrate that a regularized process of growth is inherent in the concept. We are inclined to agree with Claude's skepticism. Nevertheless, Mitrany's assumptions about politics, progress and the challenge presented by technology give functionalism a cogency which Claude's arguments do not easily brush aside. Nor does he suggest that it should. If one grants that the total breakdown of modern civilization is undesirable, a true paradox, as Mitrany suggests, seems to pervade our time.

The meaning and value of the nation-state really does seem to be called into question in the modern world. That the nation-state continues to exist and to act in time, and that groups still aspire to a state of their own is, by Mitrany's analysis, secondary to the fact that the state no longer fulfills the ends by which it justifies itself.

Mitrany's solution to this problem is that the nations should constitute spiritual or cultural entities for the most part unrelated to the satisfaction of material needs. Mitrany suggests that cultural life should be spun off from the state in much the same way that religion was disestablished by liberalism.[1] Morgenthau, we note, questioned whether this could be done without a universal political power.

Claude legitimately points out that such a project requires more agreement about the relation between the economic freedom and the welfare state than currently exist at the national level in the U.S., to say nothing of the global level of political relations. Mitrany assumes that people are irreversibly committed to trading their economic and some of their political rights in return for economic security. Though Mitrany makes a good case for this assumption it is empirically impossible to prove that that commitment is permanent. Nor can we say that that should be the case. Yet the unhampered development of technology still creates social problems which are not simply amenable to national solutions. States cannot defend themselves from nuclear-armed missiles; commerce and communication are universal.

What seems to be in question is the meaning and nature of universal society. Morgenthau does not address this question. He says that one of the purposes of politics is to defend the way of life of a community, yet does not really investigate anywhere whether the functional project is compatible with the existence of truly distinctive ways of life. Since, in Morgenthau's realism, institutions reflect and channel social forces, one might presume that whenever a particular way of life is interfered with beyond the point of endurance adjustments will be made in the institutions. Yet, as institutions become more supranational, it may be wondered whether distinctive ways of life will remain. Mitrany does not specifically discuss supranational institutions. He discusses functional activities. There is nothing incompatible between the thought of Morgenthau and the thought of Mitrany though Morgenthau's emphasis on supranationalism indicates a greater expectation that political control of the territorial distribution of social groups will still be necessary in the future.

Claude, in *Power and International Relations,* indicates a preference for collective security over the balance of power and a world state as a mode of organizing power.[2] This preference seems to tie in with Claude's general skepticism about functionalism. Since an effective collective security system presupposes a great number of moral similarities[3] its preconditions are very similar to those of the world state. Nevertheless it relies more on self-restraint than restraint by superiors. Whether substantive national and political differences, and excellences derived from them, exist in an effective collective security system, it is impossible to say. Presumably functional international organization and institution-building may reinforce, but not replace, the responsibilities of states in a collective security system. Universal responsibility on the part of states seems preferable to an indifferent cosmopolitanism.

Sewell objected precisely to the sense of indifferent cosmopolitanism which he sees in Mitrany. The irrational forces on which the notion and activities of citizenship rest are destroyed by functional rationality and there is no community in a functional world. Haas, on the other hand, had no objections to a functional world. He was not concerned with any normative judgments. Haas was concerned to see if functionalism might offer the key to getting past realist political analysis and, in the process, offer a means of predicting, scientifically, future events. Again, the fate of the particulars is of little substantive importance for Haas.

I
REINHOLD NIEBUHR AND THE WORK OF THE SPIRIT

Reinhold Niebuhr said of *A Working Peace System* that it is "the best I've ever seen on the subject."[4] The statement is consonant with Niebuhr's general conclusion in *The Nature and Destiny of Man* that man must seek to fashion some form of a common life of mankind.[5] Yet, this conclusion is not as easy for Niebuhr as for Mitrany. In fact, Niebuhr raises a question of the spirit which is not addressed by the other commentators. He does this in the context of an essay called "The Tower of Babel" in his collection of essays entitled *Beyond Tragedy*.[6]

The "Tower of Babel" constitutes a commentary on Genesis 11:1-9 which itself recounts a tale about an incomplete temple which excited the imagination of surrounding desert people. The immediate purpose of the story is to mythologically explain the source of the world's multiplicity of languages and cultures. But, "Neither its doubtful origin nor the fantastic character of its purported history will obscure its essential message to those who are wise enough to discern the *permanently* valid insights in primitive imagination."[7]

What are the "permanently valid insights" of which Niebuhr speaks? The Babel myth is equivalent to the Promethean myth. Both speak of a God, "jealous of man's ambitions, achievements, and pretensions."[8] Modern man and his rationalism see no validity in a jealous God. "Yet the idea of a jealous God expresses a permanently valid sense of guilt in all human striving."[9] Religion is not consciousness of our highest social values,[10] rather a man of true religion is uneasy with the knowledge that the "God whom it worships transcends the limits of finite man while this same man is constantly tempted to forget the finiteness of his cultures and civilization and to pretend a finality for them which they do not have. *Every civilization and every culture is thus a Tower of Babel.*"[11]

This pretension may be traced to a "profound and ineradicable difficulty in all human spirituality."[12] Man is mortal but pretends to be immortal. He is conditioned by his immediate circumstances but since he touches the fringes of the eternal he is "not merely the prisoner of time and place."[13] Man is not content to be simply a member of a nationality or any other autonomous group but wishes to be a *man*. He seeks the truth and tries to comprehend the meaning of all cultures so that he may not be trapped in his own. The essence of this seeking is the necessary creation of towers, yet, "it is also inevitable that these should be Towers of Babel."[14] The higher the tower that human imagination builds, "the more certain it will be to defy necessary and inevitable limitations."[15] The more substantial this achievement the greater the pride and therefore the sin.

The pride is not harmless, for the failure to understand man's limits leads man into tragic self-destruction. The city-state of Plato and Aristotle was not a final or perfect social organization, for it was flawed by slavery.[16] Rome sanctified with stoicism the imperfect justice of Roman law. Medieval Christian civilization was flawed by the weaving of "the peculiar economic interests of feudal aristocrats into the fabric of Christian idealism,"[17] and the just price aided the aristocrats at the expense of the producer artisans.

Furthermore, the character of a Tower of Babel is that "its always tragic history" is marked by the inability to see the flaws from the inside. The bourgeoisie destroyed feudalism, but the aristocratic classes never admitted the justice of the businessman's cause.[18] The bourgeois society replaced feudalism only to erect a new tower on the foundations of reason and science. Their presuppositionless science and ideals of liberty, equality, and fraternity understood as natural laws gave a universalism to their ideals which merely covered up their own interests and perspectives:

> The unconscious corruption of libertarian ideals, (Locke and Property) in the early and more idealistic period of bourgeois society, became a conscious corruption in its later and more decadent period, when the struggling merchants and industrialists of the eighteenth century had become the oligarchs of the twentieth-century society and conceived liberty to mean the freedom of economic power to express itself without the restraint of government.[19]

Furthermore, the impartial scientist now plays the role of the medieval priest. Even the physical scientist "may not be completely immune to the temptation of insinuating unexamined presuppositions into his inductions."[20]

In our period the industrial worker assumes the former role of the bourgeoisie behind his characteristic philosophy, Marxism, which "brings the Tower of Babel character of all civilizations into the open and makes men conscious of it."[21] Yet having recognized the finite economic and social character of all civilizations, it constructs a Tower of its own, in the perfect balancing of all human interests in a classless society.[22] It is blind to human finiteness. This blindness is evident in the Stakhanov movement which replaces religion by work as a demonstration of, and increase in, the power of man. To Marxists, "Man can learn everything and conquer everything."[23] Bourgeois rationalism wanted to destroy religion because it had built a Tower of Babel, while proletarian rationalism seeks to destroy religion because it tends to prevent man from building such a tower. The lesson is that "every form of human culture . . . is subject to the same corruption."[24]

The most pathetic aspect of this is that each civilization makes its greatest claims at the moment when the decay which leads to death has begun. It claims immortality when its mortality is in progress. The Egyptian pyramids, the Platonic city state, the Justinian code, and Thomistic thought are typical examples of this observation. The League of Nations which, as the characteristic expression of the universalistic dream of bourgeois society, moved into its new building just in time to listen to Haile Sellassi's appeal for help (which was not forthcoming), was an equally typical example. Just as the woods of autumn so with civilization; "life defies death in a glorious pageantry of color."[25]

Returning to the myth, the "diversity of languages is a perpetual reminder to proud men that their most perfect temples of the spirit are touched by finiteness."[26] Language is the earthen vessel of the "treasures of the spirit," but it is fundamentally irrational and "grounded in contingencies of nature and history."[27] Out of an utter timeliness of language come the timeless transcendence of Shakespeare, Cervantes and Goethe. "The universal notes in the world's literature are overtones. The multiplicity of languages remains. . . . The dream of a universal language and universal culture is rationalism's penchant for Towers of Babel."[28]

Biblical religion, in contrast with culture, always recognizes that a gulf remains between Creator and creature and the "Every revelation of the divine is relativised by the finite mind which comprehends it. . . . The worship of such a God leads to contrition . . . ," and " . . . a sense of guilt for the inevitable and inescapable pride involved in every human enterprise."[29]

This contrition is probably not sufficient to preserve the projects of collectivities from periodic catastrophes, for collectivities are incapable of knowing their own limits, while an individual is capable of such contrition. Further, even individuals who understand their limits do not overcome them. "That man faces an inescapable dilemma in the Tower of Babel, gives the profoundest versions of the Christian religion a supermoral quality."[30] There are sins involved "in the most perfect moral achievements,"[31] and "The relevance of this element in Christianity to the ultimate problem of human spirituality has been beyond the ken of modern man, precisely because modern man is a rationalist who builds Towers of Babel without knowing it."[32] The insight is "too profound for modernity's superficial intelligence."[33]

Niebuhr indicates that the dream of world community is essentially infected with sin. Yet we need not look far to find a counter position in Niebuhr's thought, in *The Children of Light and the Children of Darkness:*

> The Christian faith finds the final clue to the meaning of life and history in the Christ who goodness is at once the virtue which man ought, but does not, achieve in history, and the revelation of a divine mercy which understands and resolves the perpetual contradictions of human achievements. From the standpoint of such faith it is possible to deal with the ultimate social problem of human history: the creation of community in world dimensions. The insistence of the Christian faith that the love of Christ is the final norm of human existence must express itself socially in unwillingness to stop short of the whole human community in expressing our sense of moral responsibility for the life and welfare of others. The understanding of the Christian faith that the highest achievements of human life are infected with sinful corruption will help men to be prepared for new corruptiveness of the level of world community which drives simpler idealists to despair. The hope of Christian faith that the divine power which bears history can complete what even the highest human striving must leave incomplete, and can purify the corruptions which appear in even the purest human aspirations, is an indispensable prerequisite for diligent fulfillment of our historic tasks.[34]

Niebuhr seems to place man in a position of permanent tension between the universal and the parochial. "The Tower of Babel" ends on a thoroughly pessimistic note. The dream of a universal culture is the failure of rationalism, both Marxist and liberal, to gauge its own limitations. The profound sense of guilt which accompanies the recognition that to understand the limits of human intelligence is not to overcome those limits is "an insight too profound for modernity's superficial intelligence." Yet, in 1944, Niebuhr considered the building of a universal culture to be man's final possibility and impossibility. Man can and must strive for a universal culture, yet he also asserts that universal culture can be brought into being only by the spirit, and therefore, that the success of the project rests, in the final analysis, on faith.

Niebuhr's faith in a universal society was not entirely a post-war confidence. Though much more tentative, he concluded *The Nature and Destiny of Man* with the assertion that it is man's duty to build a common civilization.

The idea of a universal culture or a world government is not a natural or inevitable *telos* which gives meaning to the whole historical process, yet the technical unification of the world brings all cultures, empires and nations into a greater intimacy and contiguity which places political man under the obligation of elaborating political instruments which will make such "new intimacy and interdependence sufferable."[35] Western civilization may not have the resources to transcend national parochialism, but, "standing inside such a civilization our responsibilities are obvious. We must seek to fashion our common life to conform more nearly to the brotherhood of the kingdom of God."[36] Any failure to do so can take understanding and consolation from the Christian faith.

There is a consistent connection between the Niebuhr of *Beyond Tragedy* and the Niebuhr of *The Children of Light and the Children of Darkness.* Niebuhr contends that history, on the heels of modern Western philosophy, both liberal and Marxist, has established the possibility—and since human brotherhood is the moral dictate of Christianity, the duty—to create a universal civilization. Universal civilization may *not* be the *telos* of man, but since the God of man and history has brought us to this possibility and given us the ideal of Christian brotherhood, that objective is the task of our age. Man himself cannot complete this objective; only the spirit can. A genuine faith protects against the sin of pride and warns us that any universal civilization will be essentially defective, and that such a civilization cannot legitimately emerge from an ideology of the progress of history. "It is equally obvious," says Niebuhr, "that history does not solve the basic problems of human existence but reveals them on progressively new levels."[37] The Christian faith permits us to accept any faults and failures through the promise of the resurrection. While the immortality of the soul may let us distance ourselves too far from history and other men, the resurrection keeps the faithful in essential relation with the history of man.

Niebuhr seems progressive at the same time that he warns against the notion of communal salvation through history. Though' one hesitates to abstract Niebuhr's conclusions from the faith which informs them, there is a political teaching in his work which corresponds to the theological teaching. That teaching is that a false cosmopolitanism is possible which is more sinful than a true cosmopolitanism. A true cosmopolitan would seem to share completely in the life of one culture, yet also rise above it to a higher plane of intellectual existence. A false cosmopolitan would seem to acknowledge no essential differences, moral or practical, between his society and other societies. In one sense, the difference between the two might be compared to that between a translator of Goethe and the tourist (without intending to demean all tourists). Niebuhr says that it is the work of spirit to raise man's vision upward rather than letting it sink into indifference. The nations heretofore have found their universality in the works of single poets such as Shakespeare and Goethe. The technical unification of the world can perhaps be made tolerable, but short of the intervention of spirit, that tolerability is the sum of possible human achievement.

In one sense Niebuhr's argument intersects with Mitrany's. Mitrany's chief concern is the unification of the world by technology and the democratic revolution in social values. Writing from a somewhat different conceptualization of spirit, Mitrany says that national spirit must be released from the confining structure of the state. If Mitrany is speaking of a national separation from the state which coincides with a positive tolerance, Niebuhr and Mitrany have much the same prospect in mind. If, however, the spirit Mitrany speaks of is simply indifference created by material satiation he and Niebuhr have different prospects in mind. For Niebuhr, economic and political activity may help to create conditions for the reconciliation of nations, but that reconciliation must either preserve the nations in tolerable (though neither natural nor inevitable) equipoise, or depend on the intervention of an active spirit.

A line of argument which Niebuhr could have taken from the "Tower of Babel" story would have followed an older understanding that the separation of mankind into different communities is natural or, in terms of the story, decreed by God. Rationalism would have sinned attempting to deny or overcome a primordial decree of God. Even if God has given man a moral dictate of brotherhood this can only be effective within the earthly limits of man's estate. The seeming contradictions between brotherly love and national divisions might be resolved in the restraint by which a community treats its neighbors, not as subhuman, but as peaceful children of God—to the extent that they do not attempt to deny that status to one's own society. What Niebuhr does not analyze is the possibility that the effort to make a civilization or community universal may itself be a corruption of the brotherhood of mankind, or that the possibility of doing so is not justified by the fact that the techniques exist. That is, if in fact History is never completed by man the attempt to do so in modern man's sin. Evangelization of the Gospel may need to be universal. Recognition that even in war the enemy is still a creature of God may be a duty, but these are not in conflict with the separation of nations and their political forms. Thus even a universal Christian polity would be in conflict with God's order.

For Niebuhr, however, man is involved in a history which, by both his own activity and the activity of God, has made the creation of a universal civilization both a possibility and a duty. Yet Niebuhr does raise the questions of both spirit and national life in an interesting way. Niebuhr's point corresponds to the questions raised by Sewell. Niebuhr would not wish to see national life suppressed. Sewell would not wish to see citizen life suppressed. Both nationality and the feeling of citizenship rely on emotional attachments. In part, however, they are different emotions. Nationality is a subjective attachment. Citizenship is both objective and subjective. One can be required, under threat of severe punishment, to fulfill duties of citizenship at the same time one might emotionally wish to fulfill these duties. Both aim at an attachment to the community, yet the community is understood differently by the two types of attachment. The concept of the nation-state attempts to fuse the two emotional attachments though practice consistently shows imperfections. As both Claude and Sewell point out, the activities associated with citizenship by Mitrany should cease to carry any emotional attachment other than that of rational, economic self interest. Niebuhr seems to speak of an eventual sense of world citizenship on the part of a human nature transformed by faith. Until such a time the Christian must continue to act as political man or as a parochial citizen and a national.

II
FUNCTIONALISM AND THE HUMAN SPIRIT

Claude points out in his study, *National Minorities,* that the ramifications of the problem of the nations "extend to the basic issues of social and political philosophy."[38] The issue of the nation raises questions about the nature of the state, legitimacy, authority, rights and values, culture and politics, moral functions of government, and the relationship between conformity and compulsion.[39] From the standpoint of both politics and culture, Mitrany's functional solution to the problem of the nations is subject to some criticism on moral as well as practical grounds. The sense of these questions was first raised by Aristotle. In book three of the Politics, Aristotle questions precisely what constitutes a political community. He tells us that a political community does not exist as a military alliance, nor does it "exist for the sake of trade and of business relations." A state exists not "for the sake of life only but rather for the good life . . . all those . . . who are concerned about good government . . . take civic vice and virtue into their purview." Aristotle continues that

> It is manifest therefore that a state is not merely the sharing of a common locality (in Mitrany's case the world) for the purpose of preventing mutual injury and exchanging goods. These are necessary preconditions of a state's existence, yet nevertheless, even if all these conditions are present, that does not therefore make a state but a state is a partnership of families and of clans in living well, and its object is a full and independent life. At the same time this will not be realized unless the partners do inhabit one and the same locality and practice intermarriage; this indeed is the reason why family relationships have arisen throughout the states and brotherhoods and clubs for sacrificial rites and social recreations. But such organization is produced by the feeling of friendship, for friendship is the motive of social life; therefore while the object of a state is the good life, these things are means to that end . . . The political fellowship must therefore be deemed to exist for the sake of noble actions, not merely for living in common.[40]

Without explicitly agreeing with Aristotle's conclusion about political life, it is possible to see both why the problem of the nations raises such serious difficulties for political philosophy and why Mitrany is subject to criticism from individuals like Sewell. Citizenship and nationality are not the same. For Aristotle, citizenship seems to be superior to nationality. If government performs a moral function, as Aristotle indicates, and is more than just a compact regulating business relations and preserving life, it is incumbent on Mitrany to show how and where a functional world will perform the moral function of making possible both friendship and noble actions. Mitrany says that politics can be judged on the basis of standards laid down by the Greeks and that the essential standard is that of the good life. Yet Aristotle's point is that the good life does not only depend on material satisfaction and physical security, but also on friendship and noble action, and he does not seem to suggest that the moral function is simply one of culture.

We cannot reject Mitrany by quoting Aristotle, however, for other great political thinkers, such as Hobbes, flatly reject the notion that the purpose of political life is nobility and friendship.[41] Perhaps Mitrany assumes that nationality separated from government will still perform the moral functions of a political community which make happiness possible, but his concern over the collapse of morality with the rise of technical civilization indicates that he does not completely accept that assumption. Perhaps the problem lies in Mitrany's assumption that the great issues of political philosophy are dead, and that the purpose of politics and political science is to turn men to their economic self-interest and thereby make economic interest politics the model for global politics. What makes Niebuhr's seeming agreement with Mitrany interesting is the doubt that Niebuhr would accept economic satiation as the deepest object of government or of political life. Niebuhr's universal community seems to depend more on friendship and the possibility of noble or righteous action.

In any event, the purposes of government as assigned by a theorist are intricately related to the theorist's view of human nature. Mitrany is neither Aristotlian nor Hobbesian. He is a progressive, a materialist, and a pragmatist. According to Mitrany, the living together of man is analogous to the process of nature. The natural scientist, and in particular the biologist, sees not only change but development or growth. During the process of growth for a biological entity, functional organs are differentiated and act both as the agents of future growth and as the embodiments of past growth. The organism plays a analogous role in the development of nature as a whole. The analogy for man suggests that, as each man is a developing organism, he is also an organ of human society—taken as a whole. Man and society develop on the strength of the functions which he and society perform. To make clear the relation of things with respect to human living together is, on the basis of the principles of self-sustenance and growth, to isolate or see the functions which need to be performed (the problem to be solved) and to prescribe those functions.

The flux of human life is not simply alternations, but progress in the sense of growth or development. As a humanist then, Mitrany suggests that man has invented the concept of man toward which he develops. Therefore, too, his institutions may be understood as the material embodiments of that development or the objective embodiment of that development. That Mitrany does see political development in such a light is indicated when he says that "It took centuries to wean society away from human sacrifices on the altar of the gods only to see it replaced with the altar of the state; and while at times people have rebelled against the individual authority of gods and kings, they cannot rebel against their own all-providing collective deity."[42] Man has "dethroned the Gods, subdues nature and subjugated mechanical force, man is now the ruler of man."[43] That is, neither nature nor the gods determined man and his institutions. Man and his institutions are products of the progressive evolution of man. Excepting for man's eternal sociality, human being is essentially historical. In this sense, what at any point in history constitutes human being is determined by the conditions of the times. These conditions do not alternate between good and bad but progress toward the better from one period to the next.

The activities of government and political life are not related to the spiritual life of nations, but merely exist for the satisfaction of material needs. Yet, one cannot escape the impression that Mitrany considers the material needs to be more important than the life of the spirit, whether that spirit be religious as in Niebuhr, citizen as in Sewell or moral as in Aristotle. This is not to say that one can or should abandon functionalism. It is to say that functionalism, as expressed by Mitrany, may not be and perhaps should not be considered a solution to the problem of war. At best it would seem a precondition, as in Aristotle's trade and commerce, to a spiritual reconciliation. If one takes Mitrany's criteria of evaluation, it cannot be demonstrated that functionalism necessarily makes individuals (let alone rulers) happier.

Functionalism, or at least its essential premise, seems open to significant objections at the normative level, to say nothing of the general empirical question of possibility raised by most of the commentators we have examined. It may be that men will remain committed to their nation, their state, and their friendships (and the various political forms which those loyalties might take or which might structure those loyalties). Such a view does not preclude changes in the territorial *status quo*. It does suggest that territorial entities may not give way to functional entities. Our examination of several authorities indicates that there are arguments of the spirit which call into question the desirability of the functional project. Though most analysts have said that it may not be possible to separate economic functions from politics, we suggest a slightly different formulation. It may not be possible, or desirable, to separate spiritual life from material life. It is true that loyalties, both of spirit and of interest, are divisible—one sees that division continuously in daily life. It seems questionable, first, whether primary loyalties should be replaced and, secondly, whether there exists any neat line of separation between the spiritual and the material in the human animal. Niebuhr, in spite of his position that the work of Mitrany is the best on the subject, would surely not settle for pure economic determination of the interests of spirit.

Our concern with functionalism began with its argument about, or interpretation of, international organizations and transnational relations. The argument says that international organization and transnational activity (particularly non-governmental organization) are preparing the ground for the dissolution of territorial political government. Thomas Magstadt and Peter Schotten point out in their introductory text to the study of politics that the theorists of interdependence, who claim that the intensified character of the mutual dependence among nations has transformed the basis of the international order, "postulate a somewhat similar view" to that taken by functionalism.[44] To the extent that interdependence theorists say that this activity has transformed or should transform

the international order we see no conceptual difference between
them and the functionalists. To the extent that interdependence
theorists merely say that states have to take more account of
economic and social activities in the twentieth than they did in the
nineteenth century we would see a conceptual distinction between
interdependence theory and functionalism.

The territorial state is the primary focus of political life in the
contemporary world both sociologically and legally. We see no
empirical indication that that will change, though we do not dispute the possibility that another political entity could emerge to
take its place. We would not even dispute the assertion that a
functional world is possible. We do not see a compelling reason to
adopt functionalism or interdependence as the sole guiding norm
for scholars and statesmen of goodwill.

NOTES

1. Lord Action, in the context of a discussion of political vitality, concluded that states derive strength from incorporating a multiplicity of
nations. He argues that separating nationality from the state provides
a support for liberty and therefore, the political health of the state.
When the state tries to produce unity rather than liberty, nationality
becomes the instrument of revolution and despotism, (the lengths to
which the political power will go in order to produce one people or
one nation are arbitrary and unbounded). "The presence of different
nations under the same sovereignty is similar in its effect to the
independence of the church in the state. It provides against the
servility which flourishes under the shadow of a single authority by
balancing interests, multiplying associations, and giving to the subject
the restraint and support of a combined opinion. In the same way it
promoted independence by forming definite groups of public opinion,
and by affording a great source and centre of political sentiments, and
of notions of duty not derived from sovereign will." J. E. E. D. Acton,
"Nationality," in *The History of Freedom and Other Essays,* eds. John
Neville Figgis and Reginald Vere Lawrence, (Freeport, New York:
Books for Libraries Press, Inc. 1907, Reprinted 1967), p. 289. According to Acton (pp. 270–300) a state may create political nationality but
it derives its vigor from the interaction of diverse nationalities. Rather
than combining different nations under one government, however,
Mitrany would give different governments (functionally structured) to

the same nationality. See as well the separation between nationality and citizenship drawn by A. E. Zimmern in "Nationalism and Internationalism," *American and Europe and Other Essays,* (Freeport, New York: Books for Libraries Press 1969), pp. 65–81.

2. Claude, *Power and International Relations,* p. 10.
3. Ibid., pp. 198–204.
4. Quoted in Kenneth W. Thompson, *Masters of International Thought,* p. 203.
5. Reinhold Niebuhr, *The Nature and Destiny of Man,* 2 vols., (New York: Charles Scribner's Sons, 1964), 2:314.
6. Reinhold Niebuhr, *Beyond Tragedy,* (New York: Charles Scribner's Sons, 1937).
7. Niebuhr, *Beyond Tragedy,* p. 27, emphasis added.
8. Ibid.
9. Ibid.
10. Here Niebuhr apparently criticizes the Hegelian synthesis of man and god.
11. Ibid., p. 28, emphasis added.
12. Ibid.
13. Ibid.
14. Ibid., p. 29.
15. Ibid.
16. Ibid., p. 30.
17. Ibid.
18. Ibid., p. 33.
19. Ibid., p. 35.
20. Ibid., p. 34.
21. Ibid.
22. Ibid., pp. 36–37.
23. Ibid., p. 38.
24. Ibid.
25. Ibid., p. 41.
26. Ibid., p. 42.
27. Ibid.
28. Ibid., pp. 43–44.
29. Ibid.
30. Ibid., p. 45.
31. Ibid.
32. Ibid., p. 46.
33. Ibid.
34. Reinhold Niebuhr, *Children of Light and The Children of Darkness: A Vindication of Democracy and a Critique of its Traditional Defense,* (New York: Charles Scribner's Sons, 1944).

35. Niebuhr, *Nature and Destiny,* pp. 314.
36. Ibid., p. 308.
37. Ibid., p. 320.
38. Claude, *National Minorities,* p. 3.
39. Ibid.
40. Aristotle, *Politics.*
41. Thomas Hobbes, *Leviathan,* ed., Michael Oakeshott, (New York: Macmillan Pub. Co., 1962), p. 80.
42. Mitrany, *F.T.P.*
43. Ibid.
44. Thomas M. Magstadt and Peter M. Schotten, *Understanding Politics: Ideas, Institutions, and Issues,* (New York: St. Martin's Press, 1984), p. 483.

CHAPTER FIVE

Functional Practice: The United Nations Environment Programme

The types of conclusions one draws about the possibility or the desirability of a functionally organized world determine, in part, the questions to be asked in any examination of functional practice. Mitrany's central thesis was that the democratic revolution, the economic-technological revolution and the communitarian revolution brought society to the brink either of disaster or of a new type of political life. The old forms are worn out as are the old thoughts which created those forms. The new forms, because of the flux of democratic opinion, communal desires and technology must secure the communal needs yet be more adaptable to change than the old forms were. The concept of function provides the intellectual tool by which to shape and reshape these new institutions.

There is a general concern among the writers who have chosen to examine functionalism that the theory be empirically verifiable. What the writers seem to desire out of this testing is an indication that something like a functionalist world is a practical possibility. Two aspects of functionalism make this test extremely difficult. In the first place, Mitrany is never very specific about the criteria which might define a functional organization. Secondly, Mitrany is never very specific about the way these functional organizations will fit together. Put differently, Mitrany does not take it as his purpose to describe in detail the physical appearance of a functionally organized world. Those of us who desire a more precise view of this future world are therefore required to roam the theory for criteria by which to define a functional organization or activity, and to determine whether the accumulation of such organi-

zations and activities is likely to result in a functionally organized
world.

I
CRITERIA

In his examination of foundations and of functionalism, Kenneth
W. Thompson identifies several useful criteria by which to test
functionalism. According to Thompson, functional activity is:
1) non political; 2) often non-governmental; 3) social and economic;
4) addressed to urgent problems; 5) undertaken with a problem
centered approach; and 6) dependent on the cooperation of
professionals. In addition, Thompson says that functionalism should:
1) build habits and attitudes of cooperation; 2) contribute to the
establishment of ever broader networks of functional cooperation; 3) foster transnationalism; 4) diminish or erode state sovereignty; 5) produce spillover effects.[1] From Mitrany's view of
functionalism, the essential features of functional activity seem to
be established by Thompson's third, fourth, fifth and sixth criteria
of the first list. The second group of criteria test the secondary
effects of functional activity.[2] Since Mitrany advocates the teaching of functionalism, the secondary criteria may be said to be not
only secondary results of functional activity, but also material
props to the teaching of the political scientist. Thus the criteria
are secondary in another sense. They are secondary to keeping
men's gaze on their material interests. As a part of the continuing
concern to see functionalism in practice we have chosen to test
several of the criteria against the United Nations Environment
Programme. We wish first to determine the nature of the environmental problem; secondly, to see if the approach is problem-
centered and thirdly, to see whether UNEP makes use of professionals. Finally, we wish to see if UNEP and its activity indicate
that the requirements of the first three of the secondary criteria
are being fulfilled.

II
TESTING FUNCTIONALISM

A. The Environmental Problem

The environmental problems facing men and states which arise from economic activity are, in the first instance, the concern of ecological scientists. Yet, since remedial or preventive action depends on economic and political decisions, and since a failure to address the problems might have serious repercussions for the stability of regimes and the international system, the deterioration of the environment engages the interest and attention of politicians and political scientists.

This is not the place to judge the claims either of economists or of ecologists. Our purpose here is merely to identify in broad terms the nature and implications of the problem.

Economics and ecology are intimately related if for no other reason than that, aside from labor, the possibility of existence depends on the resources of nature. Raymond Aron has pointed to a part of the problem to which environmentalism is addressed in the context of a discussion of world empire. He contended that, if population growth continues at the same rate it has been, space and the economic resources contained in that space will again assume an importance similar to that of pre-industrial territory. National populations will fight other national populations in order to assure access to resources vital to their economic well-being. Furthermore, Aron contends that at some point either the states, acting independently, or an imperial authority will impose population-control policies on people, or modern civilization will collapse from resource depletion, and, perhaps, the ravages of modern war. Aron suggested that it would be a good idea for the nations to cooperate to solve the problem though he saw no indication that they were genuinely willing to do so.[3]

But the demands of a growing population on natural resources are only a part of the environmental problem. Some environmentalists argue that even if population growth stopped today the effort to raise the rest of the world to anything like the standard of living enjoyed in the West would exhaust the resources on which that standard depends. Furthermore, that Western and Marxist economics are dedicated, not simply to maintaining their relatively high standards of material life, but to continuous expansion of their economic product indicates to some that modern economic activity is creating the conditions of its own collapse. One of the most provoking arguments of this type came in the Report to the Club of Rome, termed the *Limits to Growth*,[4] which contends that population growth needs immediate control, global product should be distributed by a central institution, and growth economics should be abandoned in favor of a no-growth orientation. Through the use of computer projections based on current rates of population, and economic growth and resource use, *Limits to Growth* suggested that man had only a few decades to reorient his economic and social system before the modern economy consumed its base.

Others have extended the no-growth discussion to a critique of the entire system of modern production, contending that modern economic life inherently uses more resources, particularly energy resources, than the earth can sustain for even a moderate length of time. Some writers, such as Nicholas Georgescu-Roegen contend that the only type of energy which man can use for an extended period of time is solar power (and in very limited quantities, hydro and wind power). However, by Georgescu-Roegen's argument, though solar energy is much more plentiful than are coal, gas, and oil, it cannot be mined in the way our current primary energy sources are mined. Furthermore, creating the technological complex needed to supply enough solar energy to maintain the current system of production would be counterproductive in its use of energy and other raw materials. Thus the modern economic system is unsustainable under any circumstance (short of a technological innovation whose theoretical base is unknown to modern science), and we should concentrate on the conceptual elaboration of, and practical preparations for, a new age. The new age would be marked less by sophisticated mechanized technology than by the informed use of the lessons of biological nature, particularly as we know them through husbandry, for our techniques of production. There is only small room for international organization in such an understanding for one of the lessons is that standardization is counterproductive to evolutionary demands.[5] The view is more in tune with the "Small is Beautiful"[6] and appropriate technologies arguments than with the centralizing arguments of *Limits to Growth.*

We may also note here the related concern over the effects of pollution on man's ability to sustain a comfortable existence. Without venturing into the discussions over what constitutes pollution it is possible to indicate the type of concern involved. Many of the byproducts of production negatively affect man either directly or indirectly. For example, chemical by-products from some production process may pose a danger to human health and life if ingested or may, if ingested by other life forms such as fish, negatively affect man's source of food or source of pleasure. Pollution has been very hard to define and the determination what, in any particular instance, constitutes a dangerous pollutant has been even more difficult. Nevertheless, there has been a significant amount of scientific inquiry into the effects of various forms of pollution not only on man directly, but on the entire balance of earth's system of physical relations. The economic problem is the cost involved in eliminating or controlling the effects of pollution (or alternately, the long term economic effects of not doing so).

The environmental problem is clearly not a single problem in the traditional functionalist sense, but a series of interrelated problems which outline a broad issue. That issue is that industrial and scientific society has altered the physical relation between man and nature. But the material progress which has marked the industrial and scientific revolution is not going to be immediately abandoned. Furthermore, the developing countries desire to share in that progress and claim that the most pertinent environment problem is their poverty. Since the industrialized countries are not, at this point, persuaded that no growth economics or an entirely new economic structure are desirable, the specific pollution problems and the extent to which public policy should address those problems are matters of continuous expert and political debate.

Different analysts seem to come to different conclusions concerning both what the problems are and how to deal with them. But in each case the arguments of environmentalists share a concern that the modern economic system with the continuing development of industrialized societies and the desire for development by non-industrial societies, creates new and important problems for man's relationship with the rest of nature. It is obvious that in a global economic system the resource/population problem creates new pressures for states. It may equally be said that where pollution problems extend beyond the territorial confines of particular states a new international problem exists.

But only some environmentalists are concerned with economic questions. There is another view, sometimes shared by those who worry about resource depletion and pollution, oftentimes not, which makes care for the environment more than a matter of self interest. With the exception of arguments such as Georgescu-Roegen's, the views outlined above seem to be more conducive toward functional organization than the latter view is, but economic self-interest is not the sole driving force of environmentalism.

B. Environmental Perspectives

David Worster's history, *Nature's Economy*[7], demonstrates this difference in perspective quite well. He identifies organistic ecology which sees man as an equal part of the whole of nature, and mechanistic ecology which sees nature as perhaps limiting man's activity, but essentially existing for the use of man.

The organicists, Worster says,

> view ecology as a means to renew the long-lost fellowship and intimacy between man and other living things. A cooperative commonwealth of world brotherhood may be worthy goals, but the task seen as more pressing today is to break down the dualism that isolates man from the rest of nature. There is no precedent in the natural community, say the new organicists, for one species to set itself up as an independent, sovereign kingdom. The idea of man's autarchy can only be a delusion, a kind of schizoid withdrawal into a make-believe world; in truth there is no escaping the ecological matrix. Once they accept the simple scientific fact of interdependence, men and women can be taught to practice a life revering ethic such as Aldo Leopold's community of citizenship—a close, worldwide relationship between mankind and his biological kin.[8]

The organicist is said to teach a life-revering ethic based on the discovery or new articulation of man's place in nature. Man should *respect,* to the extent that his own natural existence permits, the life of other creatures. Upon becoming universal, this ethic may also make possible a "cooperative commonwealth of world brother-hood," though the latter depends on the former. Worster admits that this ethic contains a certain indifference to the economic problem. A thorough-going adherence to the ethic would probably alter significantly the purposes and techniques of production and distribution, but it would also return man to a wholeness of self. A practical adoption of organicism would at least permit men to take some joy in nature and not simply see nature as the enemy or object to be subdued.

Worster contrasts this semi-"arcadian" understanding of nature with the predominant scientific understanding of the age of ecology, the economic understanding. This understanding has found that, "Energy flow could be measured at every point in its progress through the ecosystem."[9] This understanding "dove-tailed nicely with the agronomic and industrial view of nature as a storehouse of exploitable material resources."[10] The existence of this linkage between economic and ecological science exhibits itself in three main characteristics.

First, there is a congruence between economic and ecological interdependence; "The virtues of interdependence and coopera-tion take on new importance, for without them the complex indus-trial establishment would lurch like some juggernaut into the ditch."[11] And this is true of *both* prevailing social-economic systems where "The restriction of genuine 'free enterprise' is a governing ambition of the modern economy, whether one lives under a capitalist or socialist system."[12] Furthermore, " . . . interdependence today almost always gets reduced to economic terms. Cooperation is defined, and absorbed, by the functions of production and consumption— that is all we mean by social integration, and all we have time for." And in line with this coincidence of economic and environmental science, " . . . ecology, too, has become preoccupied with these values."[13]

The second characteristic of this fusion of economics and ecology is "the primacy of efficiency and productivity as human goals . . . "[14] Efficiency and productivity have recently "become still more pervasive in their social and ecological influence, as well as, increasingly, ends in themselves."[15]

The third characteristic of modern economics which now has

become fused with ecology is "the development of a managerial ethos. It has come to be a widespread assumption that neither man nor nature can long survive without direction and control by trained managers. This faith in management is one of the more significant products of technological elaboration: eventually every specialty begins to appear too complex for lay understanding. Moreover, the compulsion to improve output, to reorganize the world for the sake of ever higher economic achievements, creates a corollary reliance on social planning, personnel management, and resource engineering."[16]

In terms of the analysis of the first section, the distinction between the approaches seems to correspond to the distinction that Sewell makes between his thought and Mitrany's. Sewell expressed concern that Mitrany's functionalism was too rational and gave up too much of the human for the sake of economic management. Though more worried about the "spirit" of nature, the first view worries that too much of that spirit is given up to economic efficiency or rationality.

C. Environment and Politics

More importantly, however, these views point to the difficulty of separating the material from the spiritual in life. Neither of the aspects of the new outlook towards the environment can be satisfied with the territorial division of the world into nation-states whose primary concern is the protection of their boundaries and populations from other nation-states. For the organicists, nation-states and their competition are merely representative of man's misplaced sense of self-importance. For the mechanists, nation-states must eventually succumb to economic rationality (in this sense expressing a view similar to that of Mitrany).

If a positive purpose is served by the political separation of men, and the preservation of differences between men, it is impossible to say at what precise point the normative claims for separation should outweigh the claims for international community. Nor is it possible to say precisely when the spiritual life of man is endangered by too much emphasis on his material life. By claiming that the way man is currently organizing his material life is contrary to nature they make an effort to ground ethics in that nature.

That is, both desire a new ethical life derived from the lessons of material life. But, rather than pointing man to higher things in the way that Niebuhr does, the two views seem to result in a lowering of a man's aspirations for himself and for his species. Maurice Strong, the first executive Director of UNEP, argued that industrialized societies, in particular, needed a new concept of growth which would place fewer demands on the environment. Though no-growth policies would not be acceptable for any existing economy, Strong argues there is room for the development of a "new growth" concept. This new concept would aim less at physical growth than at increasing the degree of satisfaction man receives for his "higher needs and aspirations in the fields of culture, music, art, literature and other forms of individual self-development and fulfillment."[17] There is certainly more recognition here that moral and cultural life are valuable in themselves. Whether Strong would have us pursue such ends primarily because of economic considerations is impossible to say, though Strong does add that "These, after all, are the areas in which man achieves his highest level of growth in human terms."[18] But, if, as suggested by Niebuhr, only select individuals can rise above their parochial circumstances through art, the spiritual lives of men will still need support in parochial institutions.

Nevertheless, the popularization of these arguments has motivated political activity. Further, practical studies, in increasing number, have demonstrated both that pollution represents a serious economic and health problem, and that the resources-population nexus is becoming, and will continue to become, a more serious problem for man. Thus, the level of awareness of the problem has increased significantly over the last decade and a half at the international level. In Section D we will see how the United Nations responded to the argument that man is destroying his material abode and his ethical life in terms of the creation of the United Nations Environment Programme, paying particular attention to the founding document of UNEP and the institutional machinery which it established.

D. Institutionalizing Environmentalism

UNEP is a publicly organized agency. It is inherently a creation of the member states of the United Nations.

The functions defined for UNEP are to be a coordinator and catalyst of international and United Nations activity with respect to the environment. Its existence as an organ of the larger United Nations organization depends in the first instance on the desire of states for such a coordinator and catalyst. The United Nations gave evidence of such a desire at the 1972 Stockholm Conference on the Human Environment and in the resulting Declaration. This document begins with the Declaration proper in Chapter I; Chapter II is composed of 26 Principles, 109 Recommendations for Action, and an Action Plan. The third chapter is composed of Resolutions on Institutional and Financial Arrangements.[19]

The Resolutions on Institutional and Financial Arrangements recommended that "The General Assembly establish a Governing Council for Environmental Programmes composed of 54 members."[20] The purposes of a Governing Council, elected by the General Assembly were several. It was to promote and to provide policy guidance and coordination "to the UN system on environmental matters, to review the activities of the Executive Director of UNEP, to promote the environmental research activities of the relevant international scientific and other professional communities, to monitor the impact of environmental activities on developing countries; to review and approve annually the use of the Environment Fund."[21]

Secondly, the Declaration recommended that an Environment Secretariat be established. The Secretariat was to be "small" serving as a "Focal point for environmental action and coordination within the UN system."[22] It was to headed by an Executive Director, elected by the General Assembly on nomination of the Secretary General. He was to be responsible for substantive support to the Governing Council; coordination and review of UN system environmental programs; advice to intergovernmental bodies of the UN system on formulating and implementing environment programs; securing the cooperation of the relevant global scientific and professional communities; providing, on request, advice on international cooperation; submitting medium and long-term plans for UN programs on the environment; bringing to the attention of the G.C. "any matter which he deems to require consideration by it;" administering the environment fund; reporting to the G.C. on environment matters, and finally, performing any functions entrusted to him by the G.C.[23]

The third recommendation of the Stockholm Declaration was that a voluntary fund be established which would "enable the Governing Council to fulfill its policy guidance role for the direction and coordination of environmental activities," by financing "wholly or partly the costs of the new environmental initiatives within the United Nations systems."[24] This fund was to be used to attain the environmental objectives set forth in the action plan and subsequent necessary tasks as determined by the G.C.[25] Furthermore, the fund was supposed to encourage and use organizations outside the UN family for projects and "complementary initiatives and contributions."[26]

The final recommendation was that an Environmental Coordinating Board be created which would be chaired by the Executive Director and operate "under the auspices and within the framework of the Administrative Committee on Co-ordination."[27] In addition, the question of coordination was addressed by requesting governments and intergovernmental and nongovernmental organizations to cooperate with the UN and UNEP in ensuring co-ordination and cooperation.

With the exception of making the G.C. a body composed of 58 rather than 54 members the recommendations were approved and implemented by decision 27-2997[28] of the General Assembly thus giving birth to UNEP. Resolution 27-2997, therefore, is the formal constitution of UNEP, though a significant change in that constitution occurred in the 1978 reorganization of the social and economic functions of the UN. The change was the incorporation of the Environmental Co-ordination Board into the Administrative Committee on Coordination, making environmental coordination within the UN system a function of an ACC subcommittee, rather than an independent or substantially independent activity. As an on-going activity UNEP—through the Governing Council—reports to the General Assembly by way of the ECOSOC.[29]

The tasks of the organization, though indicated in the Resolution on Institutional and Financial Arrangements, were laid out in The Action Plan which included an environmental assessment component (evaluations and review, research, monitoring, and information exchange),[30] an environmental management component ("comprehensive planning that takes into account the side effects of man's activities")[31] and supporting measures ("measures required for the activities in the other two catagories,").[32] Support measures included education, training and public information, organizational arrangements (primarily those discussed above) and financial and other forms of assistance.[33]

The action plan constitutes only a basic outline of the tasks. Each of the three headings and their subheadings is refined more specifically in the 109 Recommendations for Action which constitute the bulk of the Stockholm Declaration. The recommendations themselves are divided into five areas, Human Settlement Management, Natural Resources Management, Pollution Generally, Marine Pollution, and Development and Environment.[34] The recommendations are not simply tasks for a single organization to perform, but are objectives for the entire UN System. This is a key point for it indicates that UNEP was not intended to execute the tasks, but to coordinate the work of the various units of the UN system with respect to environmental questions. This function distinguished it significantly from many of the technical and "non-political" units of the UN system. While UNEP was to execute some programs on its own, that was not (and is not) the primary purpose of the organization.

The principles call upon universal society to solve the problem of resource and biological degradation as a moral obligation to future generations. They also call for action and planning at the state and interstate level. Yet, they grant only to states the real authority over the implementation of the solutions to the problems. There is a clearer sense in the declaration, proper, as opposed to the principles, that man shares a common fate and a common responsibility with respect to the environment, but there is no shift in authority.

Thus, the original intention for UNEP activity, with only slight exaggeration, was that it would act as a sort of super-coordinating group with one purpose—the improvement of the environment—in mind. Perhaps in purely functional terms this intention implies a new level of functional activity. The multi-disciplinary nature of its activities certainly indicates as much. As the lookout for dangers to the global environment, UNEP, through its information activities, its coordinating board and its fund, was expected to act as a bird of prey on the hunt. When UNEP saw a potential problem it was to swoop in on its prey and take hold firmly. Its methods were to alert, coordinate and catalyze the global community to immediate action.

Robert Munro has perhaps explained most clearly how this

original intention has fared. He suggests that since UNEP was created, environmental considerations have come to be seen as an essential part of development, that significant scientific advances have been made in our knowledge about environmental problems, that more is known about the overall state of the environment than was known in 1972, that governments have been successful in developing action plans to deal with particular problems, and that the number of non-governmental organizations has grown significantly since Stockholm.

On the negative side, however, he notes that governments have been less than successful at transferring action plans into action, and, in spite of the growing number of NGO's, UNEP has not incorporated them into its activities to the extent either of their desire or their usefulness. Furthermore, Munro notes that as environmental problems, particularly for developing countries, have mounted, the real resources of the fund have decreased. More specifically, however, Munro contends that "the implementation of the Stockholm Action Plan was too slow,"[35] and incomplete (though the plan itself has been overtaken by new knowledge and problems). Munro maintains that UNEP "gradually became too narrowly conceived and perceived as consisting only of those activities, financed wholly or in part by the Environment Fund."[36] In addition, the Governing Council failed to establish itself as authoritative for the UN system, and became bogged down in administrative budgetary and documentation questions in lieu of problem and policy issues. "One consequence, and also initially a cause, was a decline during the decade in the number of Ministers, senior environmental policy advisors and experts in many delegations, especially those from developed countries."[37]

At the Special Session of the Governing Council, held in 1982 to commemorate Stockholm, the Executive Director, some governmental delegates, representatives of some of the UN system members and, in particular, the NGO's pointed to the above problems, and more (such as the failure of political will by governments), in lamenting the fact that UNEP had, by no means, met the expectations placed on it by the Stockholm Conference. Thus, Donald R. King, Director of the U.S. State Department's Office of Environmental Affairs, suggested privately that "UNEP has taken on too many tasks largely in response to the varying priorities of Governing Council Member States"[38]; Olli Ojala, Director of Finland's Department of Environmental Protection, blamed the "strict hierarchy of decisionmaking in the Secretariat," and Governing Council sessions filled with "book keepers' bargaining" and politics for UNEP's performance;[39] and the Executive Director specifically blamed the governments for a lack of will and financial support.[40] The NGO's, in a joint statement, declared that "Governments everywhere have failed to carry forward the spirit of Stockholm."[41] The special session report, the Nairobi Declaration, offered a reasonably sober review of the program since Stockholm, and reaffirmed its commitment to the Stockholm Plan and UNEP. The regular session of the Governing Council did the same.

That there have been problems at UNEP is also indicated by the difficulty which the Executive Director has had in recruiting and maintaining a competent staff. There are those on the staff who feel that UNEP has been more successful at holding meetings and publishing reports than actually doing something about environmental degradation. Furthermore, Nairobi is not necessarily a desirable location for staff members who possess both the expertise and the management capability which UNEP needs. Some on the staff deeply resent the style of decision-making under the current Executive Director. Finally, as the *International Wildlife Magazine* has concluded, "UNEP ... inevitably shares frailties of its parent organization: the UN politicking, bureaucratic inertia, interagency friction, lack of muscle and anaemic financing."[42]

Yet, the problems of UNEP are not simply the result of the failures cited above. The many projects which King pointed to are not solely the result of the importation of Third World development issues into UNEP programming. Certainly, this is a part of the problem, and those in the West who made the argument in the late 1960s had a point in suggesting that the West's environmental problems are better handled by Western countries. Nevertheless, problems such as deforestation in tropical areas have potential consequences for the global atmosphere. In this instance, as in others, the development problem really does interact with the environmental question. It seems that, conceptually and practically, the environment is limitless, though many specific problems within the environment are geographically limited. Thus, the interest in UNEP by the governments invariably will be related to each government's most pressing environmental concern. Finally, even if all the techniques were known which would solve the man/nature question, governments would have to have, not only the will, but the capacity to implement these solutions. Arguably, a large number of governments do not currently possess that capacity.

Thus, UNEP was originally structured to offer an institutional means by which a problem identifying and problem solving approach could be implemented. Furthermore, the Stockholm action plan, the priority and functional area approach, the coordinating and catalyzing mandate and the purposes of the fund indicate a problem solving approach. Whether the problems are solved is another question which many would answer in the negative. Finally, it seems that UNEP depends on the cooperation of experts to define the problem and professionals to implement the proposed solutions. Whether they produce significant results is open to question, but UNEP is continuously using experts in various fields for conferences, studies and, in cooperation with other agencies and governments, professionals for program implementation.

The large number of other public, private and combined public and private activities going on with respect to the environment provide support for the contention that UNEP, in intention and in practice, is a functional institution. In functional terms it should be the capstone of the local, regional and inter-regional activity relating to the environment. The nature of the field is such that many environmental problems are local or regional, but not necessarily local or regional in terms of usual political boundaries. The regional seas program which UNEP maintains is not in any sense coextensive with the U.N. Regional Commissions. The Mediterranean project includes countries from the Economic Commission for Europe, the Economic Commission for Africa and the Economic Commission for Western Asia. The movement of acid rain in Europe does not take account of the Cold War. Cutting forests affects the local soil and water run-off, but also may affect the oxygen content of the atmosphere. Each specific problem would presumably call forth the institutional activity communsurate with the range of that problem. Whether UNEP, in fact, serves as a capstone and grand coordinator to the other activities is doubtful, but that is its mission.

E. UNEP and the Secondary Criteria

The secondary criteria ask whether UNEP builds habits of cooperation, contributes to networks of cooperation, fosters transnationalism and undermines state sovereignty. Certainly UNEP's
structure and mandate envision it performing each of these objectives except the last. From the standpoint of coordination, one
could point to the Mediterranean program which involves both
Arab States and Israel in mutual activity aimed at cleaning the
Mediterranean (though beyond that sphere there has been no
lessening of tensions between them). But only history can answer
this question, and UNEP's history has not spanned even a generation.
UNEP has, since its inception, been involved in the establishment
of several transnational environmental activities such as regional
seas programs, monitoring programs, multinational educational
programs and others. It undertakes programs with NGO's and
IGO's. Thus, a good case can be made that UNEP has, in reference
to perceived needs, created broader networks of cooperation in
the UN system, among governments, and among other public and
private agencies. Considering, also, UNEP's concern for NGO's, a
good argument can thus be made that UNEP fosters transnationalism.

UNEP, however, does not attempt to undermine state sovereignty.
The claim of Mitrany was that the division of man by political
arrangements has been made obsolete by developments in science,
technology and commerce; and, within limits, by the conception
of man himself in terms of human rights (in most cases understood
as economic rights). The founding document of UNEP and the
institution itself, does not follow up specifically on Mitrany's suggestions for functional arrangements—if it did it would arrange
work on problems with no "thought" to territorial boundaries.
Rather, it would have applied itself only to the extension and
intension of the problem at hand. But, there runs through all
current public organization, and the declaration and principles
reflect this fact, a fundamental reliance on governments.

Here we may usefully call on the analysis of "functional" activity offered by Maurice Strong, the first Executive Director of
UNEP. He contended, as he attempted to get the Conference off
the ground, and as he attempted to get the new agency in working
order, that the problem to be solved was not how to get nations to
give up their sovereignty but rather how to persuade them to

exercise their sovereignty collectively in order to serve a useful function.[43] In short, the fundamental reality of the nation-state prevents the success of any international activity which does not take into account the question of territoriality. Strong, was, in a sense, looking for a form of environmental collective security.[44] Mitrany's view of the pooling of sovereignty would seem to be that, to the extent that pooling sovereignty was a useful notion, that usefulness lay in what it covered up—the notion of states actively engaging in common efforts—not in the concept itself. A strict Mitranian analysis of the declaration and principles might not be impressed by the creation of a governmental agency but would be impressed if that agency was granted sufficient authority to perform its tasks. In this sense, Strong preaches a slightly revised version of functionalism.

We may describe the revision in this way. International activities may be addressed by private groups with a certain degree of effectiveness. Nevertheless, governments can not only put an end to or impede this activity, but at times possess the power, authority, and organizational capacity to do these tasks more effectively. Therefore, although it is the functional activity—in the sense of fitting the activity to the range and depth of the problem—which Strong aims at, he recognizes the desirability of encouraging the governments to take the organization of activity under their own wing and to keep it there. The gradual loss or erosion of sovereignty does not seem to be envisioned by Strong. In a strict sense, the view of Mitrany's functionalism must be that such an approach is inadequate, for, in some cases, the relation of authority to function is inadequate. But, it is this question of authority or capacity which seems crucial for Mitrany. Currently, only public authorities can create international public authorities. The functional question is not one of public versus private authority, but concerns whether the authority has capacities adequate to the performance of the tasks it is assigned.

With some fear of undermining their sovereignty, governments have been engaging in common activity since international organization began to emerge in the 19th century.[45] Such activity is, in part, political in the sense that Mitrany objects to the political as territorial states. The 26 principles make clear that UNEP will help the states. But does that mean that the activity of UNEP is not functional?

The articulation of functionalism usually offered by David Mitrany does not strictly apply to UNEP. The declaration and principles approach the functional notion, but strictly understood, authority is not commensurate with the mandate. Furthermore, bringing sovereignties together is not directly functional if it does not create nonterritorial authority. As we noted in our discussion in Chapter One, Mitrany's argument is not directed against public authority as such. It is directed against state conceptualizations of that authority. But, if the purpose of an agency describes a need of the states, the agency *is functional for the states.* We would then say that the agency is functional (but not thoroughly functionalist) even if it doesn't grant authority commensurate with responsibility to the agency. It might be argued that if it performs its function well that in the long term it might do so, but that is neither the purpose nor the reality of UNEP at present. At most, UNEP aims at persuading states to engage in self-limitation with respect to certain ways in which sovereignty can be exercised. UNEP's arguments here are not those of duty but of self-interest. Strong, as we have noted, spoke of bringing sovereignties together for the sake of mutual benefit. UNEP's program difficulties and the continuous assertion by many states of their absolute sovereignty over the use of their natural resources indicate that this task is easier said than done. Nevertheless, UNEP has engaged states in mutual activity and has been helpful in establishing both environmental conventions and environmental components in conventions relating to other subjects.

This examination of UNEP has not conclusively validated or invalidated Mitrany's argument. It has suggested that defining a problem and creating ways to deal with it are not simple tasks, but it has not shown that it cannot be done. Nor has it shown that the types of transnational and intergovernmental cooperation which arise out of functional organization are destined either to continue or to evaporate. This examination has suggested that states continue to be jealous of their perogatives, but Mitrany always granted as much. Thus, the most important conclusion this study suggests about the fate of functionalism it is that Mitrany was not wrong in thinking that his theory needed to be both descriptive and prescriptive.

NOTES

1. Thompson, *Ethics, Functionalism and Power,* pp. 96–102. The testing of functionalism in its specifically Mitranian sense does not occur with great frequency. Sewell tested functionalism against United Nations development assistance in *Functionalism and World Politics,* Haas tested functionalism against the ILO in *Beyond the Nation-State,* Claude and Morgenthau tested functionalism against the specialized agencies of the United Nations (Morgenthau also tested NATO and the EC). See Claude, *Swords Into Plowshares,* and Morgenthau, *Politics Among Nations.* Claude additionally tested the short term prospects for functionalism in "Functionalism and Conflict Resolution," paper presented at Conference on Functionalism, November 20–24, 1969, Villa Serbelloni, Bellagio. Groom and Taylor provide several different tests of the theory in *Functionalism: Theory and Practice in International Relations.* One might also examine J. Boyan Callestio and Harold Burnham "Eurocontrol: A Reappraisal of Functional Integration" *Journal of Common Market Studies* XIII, 4, Jan. 1975, p. 348; and Karen A. Mingst "Functionalist and Regime Perspective: The Case of Rhine River Cooperation," *Journal of Common Market Studies* XX, 2, Dec. 1981, pp. 161–174. In addition, the groups mentioned in the introduction and chapter 1 test functionalism in varying degrees. See Introduction, note 18 and Chapter 1, notes 3, 5 and 8. The neo-functionalists tested throughout the 1960's the prospects for regional integration, a good review of which may be found in Ernst Haas, "The Study of Regional Integration: Reflections on the Joy and Anguish of Pre-theorizing" in *Regional Politics and World Order,* Richard Falk, Saul Mendlovitz, eds., (San Francisco: W. H. Freeman and Co., 1973), pp. 103–130. See as well Ernst Haas, *The Obsolescence of Regional Integration Theory,* (Berkeley: Institute of International Studies, University of California). In the entire literature there is no evidence that what we have traditionally understood to be the character of international politics is rapidly being changed. With considerable qualification we might say that politics still interferes with functional cooperation. From Mitrany's perspective, however, testing functionalism would seem to be secondary to the political science tasks of showing men how they *should* deal with current problems and of elaborating for practical men the social "relation of things." Be that as it may, we regard the testing of functionalism to be at least one way of keeping in touch with the "relation of things." Since we find the criteria elaborated by Thompson (with minor editing on our part) to be the most appropriate for our purposes we have chosen to incorporate them into our analysis of United Nations activity with respect to

the deteriorating environment. For a more indepth examination of
UNEP and Functionalism see John Eastby, *The Political Approach of
David Mitrany: Functionalism in Theory and Practice.* Unpublished
dissertation (Charlottesville, University of Virginia, 1984)

2. We have chosen not to test the non-political and non-governmental
criteria in relation to UNEP. In doing so we do not mean to imply that
functional activity must be political and governmental. The non-
political in this context indicated the non-controversial or the technical (on the assumption that technicalities are non-controversial and
can be "worked out"). While Mitrany clearly indicates an initial
preference for the non-political, and technical services are often less
controversial, his larger emphasis seems to be more that the function
should be a service which people can agree should be performed. In
his *Ethics, Functionalism and Power* as well as other writings such as
Foreign Assistance: A View From the Private Sector, Thompson
suggests that private activities are often superior to governmental
activities in that there is more flexibility in program development, a
capacity to concentrate resources in vital sectors, fewer nationalist
fears of manipulation and fewer of the rigidities of communication
encountered with governmental programs. Most importantly he argues
that international crises are avoided in private activity because the
prestige of two governments is not at stake. Private groups should be
and usually are ready to leave on short notice if the government tires
of their work.

My decision not to test UNEP for its non-governmental character
is in part obvious—UNEP is clearly an organ of an intergovernmental
organization. The other part of the reason is important, however.
Mitrany argues that at some point effective, if not nominal, authority
over the performance of universal functions should be organized by
function, not by geography. Since for Mitrany there is no principled
distinction between the public and the private—only one of efficacy—
functional authority will often be public. The only way one can move
from territorial organization to functional organization in the public
sphere (to the extent that it is identified as such by Mitrany) is
through intergovernmental organization. That much groundwork
can be laid by private or transnational activity should not, however, be considered alien to Mitrany's thought. Presumably, in the
functional organism semi-private activities will continue in considerable measure.

In line with the public nature of UNEP it is clear as well that, for it
to do anything at all in its field, it requires the internal and external
cooperation of professionals. Thus the test for practical problem
solving answers at the same time the question about professionalism.

Finally, it will be noticed that the major thrust of the examination of the secondary criteria is with the question of undermining sovereignty. In line with Mitrany's hostility to static, territorial authority this seems to be the essential element of his political solution. It will further be noticed that spillover is not examined. While Mitrany is not opposed to success in one area of activity giving rise to other areas, to say that the state is gradually being undermined indicates much the same content as the concept spillover. Perhaps a broader examination would, however, separate the two conceptually and pursue more vigorously the extent to which performance of a function in one area requires renewed attention to other areas.

3. See Raymond Aron, *Peace and War: A Theory of International Relations* Trans. Richard Howard and Annette Baker Fox (Garden City, N.Y.: Doubleday, 1966).

4. Donella Meadow, et. al., *The Limits to Growth: A Report for the Club of Romis Project on the Predicament of Mankind* (New York: Universe, 1972). For other readable accounts, with varying interpretations of the environmental crisis see Bary Commoner, *The Closing Circle* (New York: Knopf, 1971); John Kenneth Galbraith, *Economics and Public Purpose* (New York: Times Mirror, 1973); Edward Goldsmith, et. al., *A Blueprint for Survival* (Boston: Houghton Mifflin, 1972); Mihjlo Mesarovic and Eduard Pestel, *Mankind at the Turning Point: The Second Report to the Club of Rome,* (New York: Times Mirror, 1974); *North-South: A Program for Survival: Report of the Independent Commission on International Development Issues Under the Chairmanship of Willy Brandt,* (Cambridge: MIT Press, 1980), Chapter 6; Jeremy Rifkin and Ted Howard, *Entropy: A New World View,* (New York: Bantam Books, 1980); Soedjatmoko, "Managing the Global Commons," *Mazingira* 6, 2, 1982, pp. 32–39; Barbara Ward and Rene Dubos, *Only One Earth* (New York: W. W. Norton, 1972). Wassily Leontief concludes that the greatest barrier to solving environment/production problems is rooted in the lack of political cooperation, not the scarcity of resources themselves: "Environmental Disruption and the Future World Economy," *Journal of International Affairs,* 31, 2, Fall/Winter, 1977, pp. 267–274. The U.S. Government undertook an extensive survey of the environment/resources problem, the results of which may be found in Council on Environmental Quality, *The Global 2000 Report to the President: Entering the Twenty-First Century,* Gerald O. Barney, Study Director. (Washington, D.C.: Government Printing Office, 1980–81).

5. Nicholas Georgescu-Roegen, *The Entopy Law and the Economic Process* (Cambridge: Harvard University Press, 1971).

6. See E. F. Schumacher, *Small Is Beautiful.*

7. David Worster, *Nature's Economy* (Garden City, New York: Anchor/ Doubleday, 1979).

8. Ibid.

9. Josephy Wood Krutch, quoted in David Worster, *Nature's Economy*, pp. 303–304.

10. Ibid., p. 304.

11. Ibid., p. 293.

12. Ibid.

13. Ibid.

14. Ibid.

15. Ibid., p. 294.

16. Ibid.

17. Maurice F. Strong, "Notes For Introductory Remarks" *Pacem In Terris IV*, p. 6.

18. Ibid.

19. United Nations Environment Programme, *In Defense of the Earth* (Nairobi: United Nations Environment Programme, 1981), pp. 39–106.

20. Ibid., p. 101.

21. Ibid., pp. 101–102.

22. Ibid., p. 102.

23. Ibid., pp. 102–103.

24. Ibid., p. 103.

25. Ibid., pp. 103–104.

26. Ibid., p. 104.

27. Ibid.

28. *Official Records of the General Assembly 27th Session Resolutions Adopted by the General Assembly*, 19 Sept.–Dec. 1972, Supplement No. 30 (A187730), p. 43.

29. Ibid.

30. UNEP, *In Defense of the Earth*, p. 98.

31. Ibid., p. 99.

32. Ibid.

33. Ibid.

34. Ibid., pp. 49–97.

35. See Robert D. Munro, "Twenty Years After Stockholm: Past Achievements and Future Issues," *Mazingira* 6, 1, 1982, p. 47.

36. Ibid., p. 48.

37. Ibid.

38. *Uniterra* 7, 2, p. 49.

39. Ibid.

40. Ibid., pp. 8, 44.

41. Ibid., p. 38.

42. Ibid., p. 50.

43. Maurice Strong, "One Year After Stockholm: An Ecological Approach," *Foreign Affairs,* 51, 4, July 1973, p. 706.
44. See Claude, *Power and International Relations,* pp. 94–149, for a concise description of political collective security. It is not clear that collective security in the environmental field would involve the use of sanctions and deterrence in the same way as political collective security. Perhaps the political analogy would be accurately described by peacekeeping (that is, concerted international action to aid states that desire assistance). Nevertheless, in light of the type of problem, the environment is said to present collective security seems a more accurate description of the sense in which states will sink or swim together. See as well the discussions on and resolutions with respect to collective economic security which took place in the 1970's.
45. See F. P. Walters, *A History of the League of Nations,* New York and London 1952. See also Percy Corbett, *The Growth of World Law,* (Princeton, N.J.: Princeton University Press), pp. 175–205.

CHAPTER SIX

Conclusion

The process of state making has spanned four hundred years in the West and shows no sign of fading in the new states of the Third World. But the process of international organization continues unabated as well. Does Mitrany's functional analysis help us to understand this paradox? It seems to do so. One dynamic factor, the desire for a more comfortable life, leads to the welfare state, but the welfare state cannot provide that comfort without cooperating with other states. Furthermore, as Mitrany notes, the world is technologically unified, which increases the interactions of individuals and states. The benefits of international organization which the economic and technological revolution stimulate provide a second dynamic factor behind both the process of state making and the process of international organization.

Is the multifunctional, territorial state the impediment to the happiness of people that Mitrany claims it is? It may be argued that the desire of people for happiness is not satisfied by material comfort. Presumably Mitrany recognizes this argument in his separation of nationality and government, but, as Sewell and Niebuhr remind us (for somewhat different reasons), this is both easier said than done, and is desirable only under specific conditions. The questions are, then, what spiritual function does the state serve, and how closely is that function intertwined with nationality, religion and ethical life?

The practical modern state, to the extent that it coincides with its ideal, centralizes material functions, nationality and ethical life. Its capacity to do so seems to rest on force, the persuasiveness of political men in their quest for honors, and economic self-interest. Heretofore the state has used its power to create, or at least channel people into, unique ways of life. These ways of life involve a complex intertwining of material and spiritual existence. The complexity of this existence suggests that the material and the spiritual are not absolute distinctions. Rather, they appear to be different directions on the same continuum of preference in human living. But, for individuals such as Niebuhr, the point at which an individual or a society rests on the continuum is of some importance. The point determines the rank of ends in a particular society, and therefore, the character of that society. Arguably the more an objective spiritual life is suppressed in favor of purely materialist principles, the more oppressive a particular society becomes. Perhaps the same can be said of the direction of society by purely spiritual principles. Thus, our concern over Mitrany's functionalism stems in part from the possibility that, in spite of his occasional protests, a functional world would be a spiritually impoverished world.

It is possible that the nature of man reacts automatically against such an eventuality. If so, it would explain the conclusion of most investigators of functional practice that international organization, at the governmental, quasi-governmental and non-governmental levels, shows no sign of transforming interstate relations in the immediate future. The argument could as easily be turned around, however, to suggest that the process of international organization is but the first step in the transformation of interstate relations. Our analysis of UNEP, and the determination that there are a limited number of problems which the states regard as truly global, fails to provide a ready answer to which of these interpretations of the phenomena of international organization is correct. Aron has argued that economic interactions do not necessarily change consciousness. Mitrany's agreement that changed consciousness also requires a teaching covers up his contention that the spirit always remains rooted in parochial circumstances. His teaching inherently devalues those parochial circumstances; whether that teaching can be successful has unfortunately not been proven or disproven by the study of UNEP.

Nevertheless, there is considerable sense in Mitrany's argument that the control of many of the economic and technological aspects of life should be co-extensive with the range of their effects.

Though UNEP, as do most intergovernmental organizations, clearly fails to achieve this control (for various reasons, not the least of which are jealous governments), its existence does indicate a partial recognition by governments that some economic and technological problems cannot be handled unilaterally. Perhaps no more should be demanded of governments in this sphere.

As Claude seems to suggest, the management of the power by which political communities protect their uniqueness perhaps belongs to a different level of state interaction which cannot be reduced to the management of economic and technological problems. We may go further and suggest that the power question is more closely identifiable with the spiritual direction of the continuum than the material, and that spiritual reconciliation is different from material cooperation.

In any case, we leave this investigation with as many questions as we had when we began. We still question whether interdependence is transforming interstate relations. Additionally, however, we have been led to wonder whether it should. The environmental problem, at least as addressed by Worster, raised objections to both the centralization of global economic functions and the emphasis of modern life on material comfort. We, ourselves, are not ready to say that the desire for material comfort should be superseded by a new spiritual relationship with nature, but the argument has been voiced in Western society and does not appear to be subsiding. In this sense, however, our investigation of the United Nations Environment Programme raises new questions about Mitrany's planned disengagement of spiritual and material life.

Finally, a question remains about the fate in a functional world of those men who heretofore have allied the command of political communities with their desire for honor. As Sewell pointed out, this is, in a sense, the political problem. Mitrany's argument that the needs of people should rule covers up the fact that, under the best of circumstances, these needs are provided for by individuals who view the practical aspect of ruling in much more individualistic terms. Even in a democracy, who should rule remains the political question. Mitrany does not seem to provide a satisfying answer to this question.